DIABETIC AIR FRYER COOKBOOK FOR BEGINNERS

The Ultimate Guide to Healthy Air Fryer Recipes to Managing Type 1 and Type 2 Diabetes | Low Fat, Low Sugar, and Low Carb Balanced Meals With 30-Day Meal Plan and Much More!

Isabella Reynolds

Table of Contents

About the Author

The culinary architect and passionate nutritionist behind the "Diabetic Air Fryer Cookbook for Beginners," is none other than Isabella Reynold. She was born into a family of home-based professional chefs. She started her culinary journey at the kitchen table, where flavors, ingredients, and the magic of food were celebrated daily.

Isabella's perspective as a nutritionist stems from her upbringing in a household where food was not merely sustenance but a vibrant expression of love and creativity. Her childhood was surrounded by the sizzle of pans, the clinking of utensils, and the aroma of spices, where she absorbed the essence of what it meant to create dishes that nourish both the body and the soul. Isabella has a firm belief that food is not just a source of sustenance, it also has the power to heal, energize, and pour delight into our lives. Her mission is to empower individuals, especially those managing diabetes, to embrace the joys of cooking while making informed, health-conscious choices. She understands the challenges that can come with dietary restrictions, and she has shown unique ways to manage diabetes without sacrificing the pleasures of the palate.

Through her deep knowledge of nutrition and her family's culinary wisdom, Isabella crafted this cookbook as a labor of love for a healthy lifestyle filled with delicacies. She wants every reader to experience the joy of preparing and savoring meals that are both diabetes-friendly and utterly delicious. Her approach is not just about recipes; it is about fostering a positive relationship with food, one that nourishes not only the body but also the spirit. As you read through the pages filled with guidance and recipes in this cookbook, know that Isabella is your culinary companion, guiding you toward a world of flavors, textures, and tastes that honor both your health and your love for good food. With her expertise and your enthusiasm, you will discover that diabetes management can be a flavorful, fulfilling, and lifelong culinary adventure.

Introduction

Are you suffering from diabetes? Whether you are born with it or recently diagnosed with it. Diabetes is a deadly condition that makes your body unable to manage the glucose level in your bloodstream. Worry not! This book, "Diabetic Air Fryer Cookbook for Beginners," is your ultimate savior. If you have ever wondered whether you could ever be able to enjoy your favorite crispy and delicious foods while keeping your blood sugar in check, this book is your answer. It will help you towards healthier eating delicious and diabetes-friendly foods. For many people, managing diabetes can feel like a daunting task, often accompanied by a misconception that flavorful and satisfying meals are now a thing of the past. However, it does not have to be that way. The innovative world of air frying is here to transform your culinary journey and prove that diabetes-friendly cooking can be both delectable and health-conscious.

So you can enjoy your favorite foods while managing your blood sugar levels. As you continue through these pages, you will discover a treasure trove of recipes specifically crafted for your air fryer. We have got you covered, from crispy and guilt-free snacks to hearty and wholesome meals. However, this cookbook is more than just a collection of recipes; it is your companion in the kitchen, providing guidance, tips, and nutritional information to help you make informed and healthy food choices. Our mission is simple: to show you that diabetes-friendly cooking can be both flavorful and fun. You will learn how to use your air fryer to its full potential, creating dishes that are not only good for your health but also a delight for your taste buds. Air frying is a cooking method that has taken the culinary world by storm. It offers a healthier alternative to traditional frying by using hot air circulation to achieve the same crispy and delightful results with a fraction of the oil. This means you can indulge in your favorite fried foods without compromising your health.

This cookbook is not just about managing diabetes but also about celebrating the joy of cooking and savoring every bite. It is about discovering that health-conscious meals can be a source of pleasure and satisfaction. So, join us on this delicious journey. So, let us continue through this guide and embark on this culinary adventure together, where diabetes management and culinary creativity come together in perfect harmony. And where crispy, flavorful, and diabetes-friendly meals await you. Let us make the most out of air frying and get ready to savor every bite and take control of your diabetes one delicious recipe at a time.

Chapter 1: Understanding Diabetes and Obesity

Diabetes and obesity are two widespread health issues that often go hand in hand, creating a challenging and interconnected health landscape. Understanding the intricate relationship between these conditions is essential not only for managing individual health but also for addressing public health challenges on a global scale. This chapter will explore the relationship between diabetes and obesity, understanding the risk factors, causes, symptoms, types, and essential eating tips to manage these conditions effectively.

Diabetes and Obesity Define

Diabetes Defined

Diabetes is caused by elevated blood sugar levels (glucose) due to either insufficient insulin production, impaired insulin function, or a combination of both. It is characterized as a chronic metabolic disorder that primarily has two types. Type 1 diabetes and type 2 diabetes.

Obesity Defined

Obesity, also known as being overweight, is caused by an excessive accumulation of body fat. It is typically measured using the body mass index (BMI), which takes into account a person's height and weight. Obesity is associated with numerous health risks, including diabetes, heart disease, stroke, certain types of cancer, and musculoskeletal disorders. *(News-Medical.net, 2023)*

The Connection between Diabetes and Obesity

Several mechanisms link the connection between diabetes-obesity:

- *Insulin Resistance:* Both diabetes and obesity promote the release of inflammatory substances, which can interfere with insulin signaling, leading to insulin resistance.
- *Fat Tissue Dysfunction:* Fat tissue, especially when expanded due to excess fat storage, becomes metabolically active and can produce hormones and inflammatory substances that impair glucose metabolism.
- *Inflammation:* Along with insulin resistance, both obesity and diabetes are associated with chronic low-grade inflammation, which can further worsen insulin resistance and impair metabolic health.
- *Genetic Factors:* Genetics plays a major role in both these conditions, and certain genetics can increase the risk of developing obesity and diabetes. *(Algoblan et al., 2014)*

Risk Factors of Diabetes and Obesity

Risk Factors for Diabetes

Several factors increase the risk of developing diabetes:

- *Family History:* If diabetes runs in your family, your risk of developing the disease is much higher.
- *Obesity:* Excess abdominal fat is a leading risk factor for type 2 diabetes.
- *Physical Inactivity:* A lifestyle with a lack of physical activity raises diabetes risk by reducing insulin sensitivity.

- *Age:* The risk of type 2 diabetes increases with age, particularly after 45.
- *Gestational Diabetes:* Women with gestational diabetes during pregnancy are at higher risk.

Risk Factors for Obesity

- *Diet:* High consumption of calorie-dense, low-nutrient foods contributes to obesity.
- *Physical Inactivity:* Lack of regular exercise and a lazy lifestyle can lead to weight gain.
- *Genetics:* Genetic factors can predispose some individuals to obesity.
- *Environment:* The environment plays a significant role, with factors like easy access to unhealthy foods and limited opportunities for physical activity contributing to obesity.

Causes and Symptoms

Causes of Diabetes

- *Type 1 Diabetes:* In this autoimmune condition, the immune system destroys insulin-producing cells in the pancreas.
- *Type 2 Diabetes:* Insulin resistance occurs when the body's cells don't respond effectively to insulin, causing the pancreas to eventually produce insufficient insulin for normal blood sugar levels.

Causes of Obesity

- *Caloric Imbalance:* Obesity is a condition that arises when a person consumes more calories than they burn over a prolonged period.
- *Genetics:* Genetic factors can influence how the body stores and uses fat.

Common Symptoms

Although diabetes and obesity are separate conditions, they have overlapping symptoms. For instance, excessive thirst and frequent urination are signs of high blood sugar levels in diabetes. When blood sugar levels are elevated, it can also cause fatigue, which is further intensified by the physical strain of obesity. *(Causes and Risk Factors | NHLBI, NIH, 2022)*

Types of Diabetes

Type 1 Diabetes

This autoimmune condition, usually diagnosed in childhood or adolescence, requires lifelong insulin therapy and cannot be prevented.

Type 2 Diabetes

Diabetes can be diagnosed in both adults and youth. It can be managed with lifestyle changes, medications, and insulin when necessary. Prevention and delay are possible through lifestyle modifications. *(Professional, n.d.)*

Eating Tips for Diabetes and Obesity

Eating Tips for Diabetes

- *Carbohydrate Control:* Monitor carbohydrate intake to manage blood sugar levels effectively.
- *Fiber-Rich Foods:* Consume fiber-rich foods like whole grains, vegetables, and legumes to help stabilize blood sugar.
- *Protein:* Include lean protein sources such as poultry, fish, tofu, and legumes in your diet.
- *Healthy Fats:* Opt for sources of healthy fats like avocados, nuts, and olive oil.
- *Portion Control:* Practice portion control to manage calorie intake. *(Uk, n.d.)*

Eating Tips for Obesity

- *Balanced Diet:* Focus on a balanced diet with a variety of nutrient-dense foods.
- *Mindful Eating:* Pay attention to hunger cues and practice mindful eating to avoid overconsumption.
- *Regular Meals:* Eat regular meals and avoid skipping them, which can lead to overeating later in the day.
- *Physical Activity:* Combine a balanced diet with regular physical activity for effective weight management.

Understanding the complex relationship between diabetes and obesity is essential for effective prevention and management. By adopting a balanced diet, regular exercise, and a proactive approach to health, individuals can work towards a healthier and more fulfilling life, regardless of their current health status. *(Food and Diet, 2016)*

Chapter 2: Managing Diabetes with the Right Diet

Managing diabetes involves a complete lifestyle transformation. Food choices play a critical role in controlling blood sugar and overall health. This chapter covers fundamental principles, including meal planning, carbohydrate counting, portion control, and mindful eating. Managing diabetes involves a complete lifestyle transformation. Food choices play a critical role in controlling blood sugar and overall health. This chapter covers fundamental principles, including meal planning, carbohydrate counting, portion control, and mindful eating.

Power of Meal Planning

Meal planning is the cornerstone of diabetes management. It allows you to take control of your diet, balance your blood sugar levels, and make informed food choices. It's essential to understand the impact of carbohydrates on blood sugar levels. Learn to identify and measure carbohydrates in your meals and snacks for better control. For balanced meals, include lean protein, whole grains, healthy fats, and plenty of vegetables. This combination helps stabilize blood sugar levels. Consistency is crucial, so try to eat your meals and snacks regularly to avoid significant fluctuations in blood sugar levels. *(Meal Planning for Managing Your Diabetes - Health Encyclopedia - University of Rochester Medical Center, n.d.)*

Building a Diabetes-Friendly Diet

Carbohydrate Management

- *Choose Complex Carbs:* Opt for whole grains like brown rice, quinoa, and whole wheat bread instead of refined grains.

- *Portion Control:* Be mindful of portion sizes to regulate carbohydrate intake.
- *Fiber Matters:* Choose fiber-rich foods like fruits, vegetables, and whole grains over refined grains to stabilize blood sugar and gain more nutrients.

Protein Sources:

- Lean Proteins: Add protein-rich foods like poultry, fish, tofu, and legumes to stabilize blood sugar and promote satiety.
- Balanced Meals: Combining carbohydrates with protein can slow down sugar absorption, reducing blood sugar spikes.

Healthy Fats:

- Choose Wisely: Opt for healthy fats sources such as avocados, nuts, seeds, and olive oil.
- Limit Saturated and Trans Fats: Minimize saturated fats found in red meat and full-fat dairy, and avoid processed foods filled with trans fat.

Meal Timing

Consistent meal timing helps regulate blood sugar levels. Include three balanced meals and healthy snacks. *(Diabetes Diet: Create Your Healthy-eating Plan, 2023)*

Portion Control and Mindful Eating

Portion control is vital for maintaining a healthy weight and managing blood sugar levels. Practice mindful eating by paying attention to hunger cues and eating slowly. Use the plate method to divide your plate into sections for different food groups. Choose nutrient-dense snacks and avoid mindless snacking.

Regular monitoring and Flexibility

Regularly monitoring your blood sugar levels is essential to gauge the impact of dietary choices.

- *Blood Sugar Testing:* Follow your healthcare provider's recommendations for blood sugar monitoring. Keep a record to identify patterns.
- *Regular Testing:* Follow your healthcare provider's recommendations for blood sugar testing.
- *Tracking Patterns:* Monitor how different foods and meals affect your blood sugar levels.
- *Consultation:* Regularly meet with your healthcare team, including a registered dietitian, to adjust your meal plan and medications as needed.
- *Adjustments:* Be prepared to adjust your diet based on your blood sugar readings. Flexibility is key to successful diabetes management. *(National Library of Medicine, n.d.)*

Chapter 3: Air Frying for Healthy Living

Air frying is a healthier way to enjoy crispy and delicious foods without excessive oil. This chapter will explore the benefits and techniques of air frying for a healthier lifestyle.

Benefits of Air frying

Reduced Oil Usage

Air frying requires significantly less oil than traditional frying methods due to hot air circulation, which can promote heart health and lower calorie consumption.

Healthier Cooking

Air frying uses less oil and preserves more nutrients than deep frying, making it a healthier option that reduces the intake of saturated fats that can cause heart disease.

Master the Hidden Air Frying Techniques:

Preparing Foods for Air Frying:

- *Dry Ingredients:* Ensure that the food you are air frying is dry. Excess moisture can prevent crisping.
- *Lightly Oil or Spray:* While you use less oil, a light spray of oil on the surface of food can enhance crispiness.

Temperature and Time Control:

- *Precision Matters:* Familiarize yourself with your air fryer's temperature and time settings for different foods.

- *Shaking and Flipping:* Occasionally shaking or flipping the food can ensure even cooking.

Cooking a Variety of Foods:

- Air fryers can cook many types of food. Try different recipes to find favorites. *(Ryan, 2023)*

Tips for Ultimate Air frying experience:

Choose Nutrient-Rich Ingredients:

Opt for whole foods, lean proteins, and plenty of vegetables to create health-conscious air-fried meals. Load up on a variety of colorful vegetables, which are rich in vitamins and minerals.

Limit Processed Foods

Air frying is healthier; however, it is also important to avoid processed food. Make your own food instead of relying on frozen options, which often contain unhealthy additives.

Mindful Seasoning

Enhance the flavor of your dishes without relying on excessive salt or sugar by experimenting with herbs, spices, and seasoning.

Use Healthy Fats Sparingly

Using cooking spray or brushing with oil are both effective techniques to add texture and flavor to your dishes. If you want a crispy coating, using cooking spray to lightly coat your food is a great option. On the other hand, brushing your food with oil can create a beautiful golden crunch that is sure to elevate your dish. With these techniques, your food will not only taste great but also look appetizing.

Air frying is more than just a cooking technique; it's a lifestyle choice that can help you achieve a healthier way of living. By adopting air frying, you can enjoy the flavors and textures you love while being mindful of your health. Whether you are aiming to reduce saturated fat, retain nutrients, or simply indulge in crispy foods without feeling guilty, air frying is a culinary innovation that perfectly complements a health-conscious lifestyle. So why not explore the possibilities and relish the delights of air frying as you journey towards better health?

BREAKFAST RECIPES

1-Healthy Vegetable Frittata

Delicious and filling, a healthy vegetable frittata is a quick and simple meal power-packed with veggies' vitamins and nutritious protein.

Preparation Time: 10 minutes

Cooking Time: 45 minutes

Servings: 4

Ingredients:

- 8 eggs
- 50 g (1/2 cup) parmesan cheese, shredded
- 67 g (1 cup) kale, chopped
- 1 medium onion, sliced
- 1 bell pepper, sliced
- 12-15 mushrooms, sliced
- 122 g (1/2 cup) unsweetened almond milk
- Pepper
- Salt

Directions:

- Preheat the air fryer to 400 F/ 200 C.
- Line the air fryer basket with parchment paper. Make sure to position of parchment paper evenly in the center to hold the frittata mixture on all sides.
- Add bell pepper, mushrooms, and onion into the air fryer basket. Season with pepper and salt.
- Air fry the vegetables for 15 minutes. Shake the basket halfway through.
- Meanwhile, in a bowl, whisk eggs with milk, cheese, pepper, and salt.
- Remove the air fryer basket from the air fryer, add kale, and stir with a spatula.
- Pour egg mixture over veggies.

- Bake at 300 F for 25-30 minutes.
- Cut into slices and serve.

Nutritional Value (Amount per Serving):

- Calories 211, Fat 12.1 g, Carbohydrates 9.7 g, Sugar 4.3 g, Protein 18 g, Cholesterol 336 mg

2-Crustless Quiche

A crustless quiche is a low-carb and gluten-free alternative to traditional quiche that's just as delicious and versatile a dish that can be enjoyed for breakfast, brunch, or even a light dinner.

Preparation Time: 10 minutes

Cooking Time: 14 minutes

Servings: 2

Ingredients:

- 1 egg yolk
- 2 eggs
- 2 tablespoons mozzarella cheese, shredded
- 2 tablespoons feta cheese, crumbled
- 18 g (¼ cup) broccoli, steamed & chopped
- 2 teaspoons fresh lime juice
- 1 tablespoon sour cream
- 60 g (¼ cup) half and half
- Pepper
- Salt

Directions:

- Grease two ramekin dishes with butter.
- Evenly divide broccoli in the prepared dishes.
- Add crumbled cheese on top of broccoli.

- In a bowl, whisk together egg yolk, eggs, lime juice, sour cream, half and half, pepper, and salt.
- Pour egg mixture evenly into the ramekins.
- Add shredded mozzarella cheese on top of each quiche.
- Place the ramekins into the air fryer basket and cook at 325 F/ 162 C for 14 minutes.
- Serve and enjoy.

Nutritional Value (Amount per Serving):

- Calories 262, Fat 18.4 g, Carbohydrates 8.1 g, Sugar 1.8 g, Protein 17.8 g, Cholesterol 306 mg

3-Veggie Egg Cups

Veggie egg cups are one of the easy and healthy options for breakfast or a snack. They are easy to make and you can change them to fit your taste by using the veggies and spices you like best.

Preparation Time: 10 minutes

Cooking Time: 12 minutes

Servings: 4

Ingredients:

- 8 eggs
- 1/8 teaspoon onion powder
- 1/8 teaspoon garlic powder
- 32 (1 cup) mixed vegetables, chopped
- 4 tablespoons parmesan cheese, shredded
- Pepper
- Salt

Directions:

- Preheat the air fryer to 300 F/ 148 C.

- Grease four ramekins with butter and set aside.
- In a bowl, whisk eggs with onion powder, garlic powder, pepper, and salt.
- Add mixed vegetables and shredded cheese and stir everything well to combine.
- Pour egg mixture into the prepared ramekins.
- Place ramekins into the air fryer basket and cook for 12 minutes.
- Serve and enjoy.

Nutritional Value (Amount per Serving):

- Calories 239, Fat 14.9 g, Carbohydrates 6.2 g, Sugar 0.7 g, Protein 21 g, Cholesterol 347 mg

4-Baked Banana Oatmeal

Baked banana oatmeal is a tasty and healthy breakfast meal made by mixing oats, ripe bananas, and a few other ingredients, together and bakes this mixture until it turns a golden brown and firms up.

Preparation Time: 10 minutes

Cooking Time: 07 minutes

Servings: 2

Ingredients:

- 1 egg
- 62 g (½ cup) oat flour
- ½ teaspoon baking soda
- 1 tablespoon maple syrup
- 1 banana, mashed
- 1/8 teaspoon cinnamon
- Pinch of salt

Directions:

- Preheat the air fryer to 300 F/ 148 C.
- Grease two ramekins with butter and set aside.
- In a bowl, mix together egg, oat flour, banana, maple syrup, baking soda, cinnamon, and salt until well combined.
- Divide the oat mixture evenly into the prepared ramekins.
- Place ramekins into the air fryer basket and cook for 7 minutes.
- Serve and enjoy.

Nutritional Value (Amount per Serving):

- Calories 201, Fat 3.9 g, Carbohydrates 36.2 g, Sugar 13.3 g, Protein 6.4 g, Cholesterol 82 mg

5-Sweet Potato Hash

Sweet potato hash is a delicious and satisfying dish created by dicing sweet potatoes and onions, along with other ingredients. It offers the flexibility to customize it according to your preferences.

Preparation Time: 10 minutes

Cooking Time: 14 minutes

Servings: 2

Ingredients:

- 1 large sweet potato, cut into ½-inch cubes
- 1 bell pepper, seeded & chopped
- 1 small onion, chopped
- 1 teaspoon paprika
- 2 tablespoons olive oil
- Pepper

- Salt

Directions:

- In a bowl, toss sweet potato, onion, bell pepper, oil, paprika, pepper, and salt to combine.
- Add sweet potato mixture into the air fryer basket and cook at 400 F/ 204 C for 14 minutes. Stir halfway through.
- Serve and enjoy.

Nutritional Value (Amount per Serving):

- Calories 237, Fat 14.5 g, Carbohydrates 27 g, Sugar 10.4 g, Protein 3 g, Cholesterol 0 mg

6-Spinach Egg Bites

Spinach egg bites are flavorful, healthful treats prepared from eggs, spinach, cheese, and spices. They offer taste and nutritional advantages, making them an easy and satisfying choice for breakfast.

Preparation Time: 10 minutes

Cooking Time: 14 minutes

Servings: 4

Ingredients:

- 5 eggs, lightly beaten
- ¼ cup feta cheese, crumbled
- ½ cup bell pepper, chopped
- 12 g (½ cup) fresh spinach, chopped
- 2 tablespoons unsweetened almond milk
- Pepper
- Salt

Directions:

- Grease four ramekins with oil and set aside.
- Preheat the air fryer to 340 F/ 171 C.
- In a bowl, whisk together eggs, milk, pepper, and salt. Add crumbled cheese, bell pepper, and spinach and stir well to combine.
- Pour egg mixture into the prepared ramekins.
- Place ramekins into the air fryer basket and cook for 12-14 minutes.
- Serve and enjoy.

Nutritional Value (Amount per Serving):

- Calories 110, Fat 7.6 g, Carbohydrates 2.2 g, Sugar 1.6 g, Protein 8.5 g, Cholesterol 213 mg

7-Perfect Oatmeal Bites

Perfect oatmeal bites are delightful, bite-sized snacks or breakfast treats that are both delicious and nutritious. These little bites are a convenient and nutritious way to satisfy your snack cravings.

Preparation Time: 10 minutes

Cooking Time: 06 minutes

Servings: 6

Ingredients:

- 180 g (2 cups) oatmeal
- 1 ripe banana, mashed
- ¼ teaspoon ground ginger
- ½ teaspoon ground nutmeg
- ½ teaspoon cinnamon
- 1 teaspoon vanilla
- 2 tablespoons honey
- 4 tablespoons unsweetened applesauce

Directions:

- Preheat the air fryer to 330 F/ 165 C.
- In a bowl, mix together oatmeal, mashed banana, ginger, nutmeg, cinnamon, vanilla, honey, and applesauce until well combined.
- Spoon the oatmeal mixture into the silicone muffin molds and place into the air fryer basket.
- Cook for 6 minutes or until the toothpick comes out clean.
- Serve and enjoy.

Nutritional Value (Amount per Serving):

- Calories 150, Fat 1.9 g, Carbohydrates 30.3 g, Sugar 9.6 g, Protein 3.9 g, Cholesterol 0 mg

8-Quick & Easy Granola

Quick and easy granola is a flexible and tasty snack or breakfast alternative that you can create at home in no time. It's a flexible and homemade snack that's healthier than store-bought ones.

Preparation Time: 05 minutes

Cooking Time: 10 minutes

Servings: 4

Ingredients:

- 81 g (1 cup) rolled oats
- 1 teaspoon vanilla
- 2 tablespoons coconut oil, melted
- 3 tablespoons honey
- 1 teaspoon cinnamon
- 70 g (½ cup) almonds, chopped
- Pinch of salt

Directions:

- Line the air fryer basket with parchment paper.
- In a bowl, mix together oats, vanilla, oil, honey, cinnamon, almonds, and salt.
- Add the oats mixture into the air fryer basket and spread evenly.
- Cook at 350 F/ 176 C for 10 minutes.
- Remove the granola from air fryer basket and let it cool completely.
- Serve and enjoy.

Nutritional Value (Amount per Serving):

- Calories 257, Fat 14.1 g, Carbohydrates 30 g, Sugar 13.8 g, Protein 5.3 g, Cholesterol 0 mg

9-Blueberry Muffins

Blueberry muffins are a delicious, sweet snack featuring juicy blueberries in a soft and moist muffin.

Preparation Time: 05 minutes

Cooking Time: 05 minutes

Servings: 6

Ingredients:

- 1 large egg
- 190 g (1 cup) blueberries
- 1 teaspoon baking powder
- ¼ cup unsweetened almond milk
- 2 tablespoons Swerve
- 96 g (1 cup) almond flour
- Pinch of salt

Directions:

- In a bowl, mix together egg, almond flour, sweetener, almond milk, baking powder, and salt until well combined.

- Add blueberries and fold well.
- Spoon batter into the silicone muffin molds and place into the air fryer basket.
- Cook at 320 F/ 160 C for 5 minutes.
- Serve and enjoy.

Nutritional Value (Amount per Serving):

- Calories 57, Fat 3.4 g, Carbohydrates 5.7 g, Sugar 2.6 g, Protein 2.3 g, Cholesterol 31 mg

10-Tasty Greek Omelet

Greek omelet is a nutritious, delicious dish made with eggs, Mediterranean-inspired ingredients, which flavors like tomatoes, feta cheese, and fresh herbs.

Preparation Time: 10 minutes

Cooking Time: 20 minutes

Servings: 2

Ingredients:

- 4 eggs
- 1 teaspoon dried oregano
- 1 onion, diced
- 100 g (½ cup) grape tomatoes, cut in half
- 50 g (½ cup) feta cheese, crumbled
- 15 g (½ cup) fresh spinach, chopped
- 3 tablespoons heavy whipping cream
- Pepper
- Salt

Directions:

- Preheat the air fryer to 350 F/ 176 C.
- Grease a 6-inch baking pan with butter and set aside.
- In a bowl, whisk together eggs, oregano, heavy whipping cream, pepper, and salt.

- Add onion, tomatoes, cheese, and spinach, and stir well.
- Pour egg mixture into the prepared baking pan.
- Cover baking pan with foil and place it into the air fryer basket.
- Cook the omelet for 12 minutes.
- Remove foil and cook for 6-8 minutes more.
- Serve and enjoy.

Nutritional Value (Amount per Serving):

- Calories 337, Fat 25.3 g, Carbohydrates 10.5 g, Sugar 5.8 g, Protein 18.2 g, Cholesterol 392 mg

APPETIZERS & SNACKS RECIPES

1-Crunchy Chickpeas

Crunchy chickpeas are a crunchy and tasty snack prepared from chickpeas, also known as garbanzo beans. They are often seasoned and roasted till they become crispy and delightful for munching on.

Preparation Time: 05 minutes

Cooking Time: 13 minutes

Servings: 4

Ingredients:

- 425 g (15 ounces) can chickpeas, rinsed, drained & pat dry with paper towels
- ¼ teaspoon onion powder
- ¼ teaspoons garlic powder
- ¼ teaspoon dried dill
- ¼ tablespoon dried parsley
- 1 tablespoon olive oil
- Pepper
- Salt

Directions:

- In a bowl, toss chickpeas with onion powder, garlic powder, dill, parsley, oil, pepper, and salt until well coated.
- Add chickpeas into the air fryer basket and cook at 400 F/ 204 C for 10-13 minutes or until crispy. Stir halfway through.
- Serve and enjoy.

Nutritional Value (Amount per Serving):

- Calories 158, Fat 4.7 g, Carbohydrates 24.4 g, Sugar 0.1 g, Protein 5.3 g, Cholesterol 0 mg

2-Roasted Cashews

Roasted cashews are a tasty and crunchy snack prepared from cashew nuts that have been seasoned and roasted until they get crispy and golden brown.

Preparation Time: 05 minutes

Cooking Time: 07 minutes

Servings: 4

Ingredients:

- 150 g (1 cup) cashews
- ½ teaspoon garlic powder
- ½ teaspoon lemon-pepper seasoning
- 1 tablespoon olive oil
- Salt

Directions:

- Preheat the air fryer to 330 F/ 165 C.
- In a bowl, toss cashews with garlic powder, lemon pepper seasoning, oil, and salt until well coated.
- Add cashews into the air fryer basket and cook for 7 minutes. Stir halfway through.
- Serve and enjoy.

Nutritional Value (Amount per Serving):

- Calories 228, Fat 19.4 g, Carbohydrates 11.6 g, Sugar 1.8 g, Protein 5.3 g, Cholesterol 0 mg

3-Crispy Potato Bites

Crispy potato bites are delicious bite-sized snacks or appetizers made from potatoes that are crispy on the outside and soft on the inside.

Preparation Time: 10 minutes

Cooking Time: 20 minutes

Servings: 6

Ingredients:

- 453 g (1 pound) potatoes, cut into small chunks
- 1 teaspoon oregano
- 1 teaspoon Greek seasoning
- 1 teaspoon lemon zest, grated
- 1 teaspoon fresh lemon juice
- 1 tablespoon olive oil
- Pepper
- Salt

Directions:

- In a bowl, toss potatoes with oregano, Greek seasoning, lemon zest, lemon juice, oil, pepper, and salt until well coated.
- Add potatoes into the air fryer basket and cook at 400 F/ 204 C for 15-20 minutes or until crispy. Stir halfway through.
- Serve and enjoy.

Nutritional Value (Amount per Serving):

- Calories 75, Fat 2.5 g, Carbohydrates 12.4 g, Sugar 0.9 g, Protein 1.4 g, Cholesterol 0 mg

4-Delicious Broccoli Tots

These broccoli tots are not only tasty but also a great way to get more greens into your diet. They are ideal for both youngsters and adults and may be offered as a healthy alternative to classic potato tots.

Preparation Time: 05 minutes

Cooking Time: 12 minutes

Servings: 24 tots

Ingredients:

- 1 egg yolk
- 1 large broccoli head, cut into florets, steam & mash using a fork
- 3 tablespoons parmesan cheese, grated
- ½ teaspoon paprika
- 2 tablespoons almond flour
- Pepper
- Salt

Directions:

- In a bowl, mix together mash broccoli, egg yolk, grated cheese, paprika, almond flour, pepper, and salt until well combined.
- Make equal shapes of tots using a broccoli mixture and place them onto a parchment-lined baking sheet and place them in the refrigerator for 10 minutes.
- Place prepared broccoli tots into the air fryer basket and cook 370 F/ 187 C for 10-12 minutes or until crispy.
- Serve and enjoy.

Nutritional Value (Amount per Serving):

- Calories 29, Fat 2.1 g, Carbohydrates 1.1 g, Sugar 0.2 g, Protein 1.9 g, Cholesterol 11 mg

5-Perfect Carrot Fries

Carrot fries are a versatile and nutritious snack or side dish that can be customized with various seasonings to suit individual tastes.

Preparation Time: 05 minutes

Cooking Time: 18 minutes

Servings: 4

Ingredients:

- 6 medium carrots, sliced into fries shapes
- ½ teaspoon paprika
- ½ teaspoon garlic powder
- 2 tablespoons olive oil
- 2 tablespoons cornstarch
- Pepper
- Salt

Directions:

- Preheat the air fryer to 390 F/ 198 C.
- In a bowl, toss carrot slices with paprika, garlic powder, oil, cornstarch, pepper, and salt until well coated.
- Add carrot fries into the air fryer basket and cook for 15-18 minutes. Shake the basket after every 6 minutes.
- Serve and enjoy.

Nutritional Value (Amount per Serving):

- Calories 115, Fat 7 g, Carbohydrates 13.1 g, Sugar 4.6 g, Protein 0.9 g, Cholesterol 0 mg

6-Spicy Sweet Potato Wedges

Carrot fries are a nutritious and satisfying snack or side dish that can be customized with various seasonings to suit your taste.

Preparation Time: 05 minutes

Cooking Time: 20 minutes

Servings: 4

Ingredients:

- 2 medium sweet potatoes, clean & cut into wedges
- ½ teaspoon cayenne
- ½ teaspoon paprika
- 2 tablespoons olive oil
- ¼ teaspoon garlic powder
- Pepper
- Salt

Directions:

- Add sweet potato wedges into the bowl and cover with cold water. Soak for 20 minutes.
- Remove sweet potato wedges from the water and place onto a baking sheet. Pat dry sweet potato wedges using paper towels.
- In a bowl, toss sweet potato wedges with cayenne, paprika, oil, garlic powder, pepper, and salt until well coated.
- Add sweet potato wedges into the air fryer basket and cook at 390 F/ 198 C for 20 minutes. Shake the basket after every 5 minutes.
- Serve and enjoy.

Nutritional Value (Amount per Serving):

- Calories 151, Fat 7.2 g, Carbohydrates 21.3 g, Sugar 0.5 g, Protein 1.3 g, Cholesterol 0 mg

7-Crispy Zucchini Fritters

Crispy zucchini fritters are one of the delicious ways to consume zucchini that can be customized with your preferred herbs and spices.

Preparation Time: 10 minutes

Cooking Time: 14 minutes

Servings: 8 fritters

Ingredients:

- 3 medium zucchini, grated & squeeze out excess liquid
- 1 tablespoon cilantro, chopped
- 1 teaspoon garlic, minced
- ½ small onion, chopped
- ¼ teaspoon chili powder
- 92 (1 cup) chickpea flour
- Salt

Directions:

- Preheat the air fryer to 350 F/ 176 C.
- Spray air fryer basket with cooking spray.
- In a bowl, mix together grated zucchini, chickpea flour, chili powder, onion, garlic, cilantro, and salt until well combined.
- Using a spoon drop the zucchini mixture into the air fryer basket and cook for 12-14 minutes. Flip halfway through.
- Serve and enjoy.

Nutritional Value (Amount per Serving):

- Calories 105, Fat 1.7 g, Carbohydrates 18.2 g, Sugar 4.2 g, Protein 5.8 g, Cholesterol 0 mg

8-Easy Hasselback Potatoes

Easy Hasselback potatoes are a wonderful side dish prepared with whole potatoes that have been partly sliced and roasted till crispy on the exterior and soft on the inside.

Preparation Time: 10 minutes

Cooking Time: 50 minutes

Servings: 4

Ingredients:

- 4 medium potatoes
- 4 tablespoons olive oil
- 1/2 teaspoon chili powder
- 1/2 teaspoon garlic powder
- Pepper
- Salt

Directions:

- Cut the potatoes crosswise into 1/8-inch thick slices, leaving the bottom intact.
- Brush potatoes with oil and sprinkle with chili powder, garlic powder, pepper, and salt.
- Place potatoes into the air fryer basket and cook at 350 F/ 176 for 35 minutes.
- Flip the potatoes and continue cooking them for an additional 15 minutes.
- Serve and enjoy.

Nutritional Value (Amount per Serving):

- Calories 269, Fat 14.3 g, Carbohydrates 33.9 g, Sugar 2.6 g, Protein 3.7 g, Cholesterol 0 mg

9-Healthy Veggie Skewers

Vegetable skewers are not only delicious but also an enjoyable and visually appealing way to enjoy a variety of vegetables.

Preparation Time: 10 minutes

Cooking Time: 08 minutes

Servings: 6

Ingredients:

- 1 small zucchini, cut into chunks
- 180 g (1 cup) grape tomatoes
- 1 medium onion, cut into chunks
- 1/2 red bell pepper, cut into chunks
- 125 g (1 cup) button mushrooms
- 2 tablespoons olive oil
- 1/2 teaspoon cumin powder
- Pepper
- Salt

Directions:

- Preheat the air fryer to 390 F/ 198.
- In a bowl, toss zucchini, tomatoes, onion, bell pepper, mushrooms, oil, cumin powder, pepper, and salt until well coated.
- Thread zucchini, onion, bell pepper, tomatoes, and mushrooms onto the soaked skewers.
- Place skewers into the air fryer basket and cook for 8 minutes. Turn halfway through.
- Serve and enjoy.

Nutritional Value (Amount per Serving):

- Calories 62, Fat 4.9 g, Carbohydrates 4.8 g, Sugar 2.6 g, Protein 1.2 g, Cholesterol 0 mg

10-Crispy Cabbage Patties

The cabbage patties are a delicious and crispy way to enjoy cabbage, which can be customized with your preferred seasonings and spices.

Preparation Time: 10 minutes

Cooking Time: 14 minutes

Servings: 4

Ingredients:

- 1 egg
- 134 g (1 1/2 cups) cabbage, grated
- 1/2 teaspoon garlic, minced
- 1 tablespoon parsley, minced
- 1 tablespoon onion, chopped
- 2 teaspoons olive oil
- 1 teaspoon ground cumin
- 1 tablespoon coconut flour
- Pepper
- Salt

Directions:

- Mix grated cabbage, egg, garlic, parsley, onion, oil, cumin, coconut flour, pepper, and salt in a bowl until well combined.
- Spray the air fryer basket with cooking spray.
- Make equal shapes of patties from the cabbage mixture and place them into the air fryer basket.
- Cook at 350 F/ 176 C for 14 minutes. Turn patties halfway through.
- Serve and enjoy.

Nutritional Value (Amount per Serving):

- Calories 54, Fat 3.8 g, Carbohydrates 3.5 g, Sugar 1.1 g, Protein 2.1 g, Cholesterol 41 mg

POULTRY RECIPES

1-Tasty Chicken Bites

Tasty chicken bites are perfectly seasoned, bite-sized pieces of chicken, ideal for dipping in sauces like ketchup, barbecue sauce, honey mustard, etc.

Preparation Time: 05 minutes

Cooking Time: 12 minutes

Servings: 2

Ingredients:

- 1 large chicken breast, skinless, boneless & cut into bite-size pieces
- ¼ teaspoon chipotle chili powder
- ½ teaspoon onion powder
- ½ teaspoon garlic powder
- 1 tablespoon olive oil
- 1 teaspoon smoked paprika
- Pepper
- Salt

Directions:

- Preheat the air fryer to 390 F/ 198 C.
- In a bowl, toss chicken pieces with chili powder, onion powder, garlic powder, oil, paprika, pepper, and salt until well coated.
- Add chicken pieces into the air fryer basket and cook for 10-12 minutes or until cooked. Shake the basket halfway through.
- Serve and enjoy.

Nutritional Value (Amount per Serving):

- Calories 133, Fat 8.6 g, Carbohydrates 1.9 g, Sugar 0.5 g, Protein 12.2 g, Cholesterol 36 mg

2-Dijon Chicken Breasts

Dijon chicken breasts are tasty and juicy chicken breasts covered in a creamy Dijon mustard sauce. This traditional recipe is easy to prepare and excellent for a fast evening dinner.

Preparation Time: 05 minutes

Cooking Time: 25 minutes

Servings: 2

Ingredients:

- 2 chicken breasts, skinless & boneless
- ¼ teaspoon garlic powder
- 1 teaspoon dried tarragon
- 2 teaspoons honey
- 1 tablespoon olive oil
- 2 tablespoons Dijon mustard
- Pepper
- Salt

Directions:

- In a bowl, mix together garlic powder, tarragon, honey, oil, Dijon mustard, pepper, and salt.
- Add chicken to the bowl and coat well with marinade. Cover bowl and place in refrigerator for 30 minutes to marinate.
- Remove chicken from refrigerator.
- Spray air fryer basket with cooking spray.
- Place marinated chicken breasts into the air fryer basket and cook at 370 F/ 187 C for 10 minutes. Flip chicken breasts and cook for 8-10 minutes more or until the internal temperature of the chicken is reaches to 165 F.
- Slice and serve.

Nutritional Value (Amount per Serving):

- Calories 371, Fat 18.5 g, Carbohydrates 7 g, Sugar 6 g, Protein 43.1 g, Cholesterol 130 mg

3-Flavorful Pesto Chicken Breasts

Flavorful pesto chicken breasts are tasty and fragrant chicken breasts that are topped with a vivid pesto sauce. This recipe is packed with the aromas of fresh basil, garlic, and Parmesan cheese.

Preparation Time: 05 minutes

Cooking Time: 15 minutes

Servings: 4

Ingredients:

- 454 g (1 pound) chicken breasts, skinless, boneless & cut into slices
- 74 g (1/3 cup) olive oil
- 22 g (¼ cup) parmesan cheese, grated
- 2 garlic cloves
- 2 tablespoons pine nuts
- 1 cup fresh basil
- Pepper
- Salt

Directions:

- Add oil, cheese, garlic, pine nuts, basil, pepper, and salt into the blender and blend until smooth.
- In a bowl, mix together pesto and chicken until well coated.
- Place chicken into the air fryer basket and cook at 400 F/ 204 C for 10 minutes.
- Flip the chicken and cook for 5 minutes more.
- Serve and enjoy.

Nutritional Value (Amount per Serving):

- Calories 398, Fat 28.6 g, Carbohydrates 1.3 g, Sugar 0.2 g, Protein 34.3 g, Cholesterol 102 mg

4-Marinated Chicken

Marinated chicken is chicken that has been marinated in a tasty mixture of ingredients to increase its taste and softness. Marinating chicken before cooking may infuse it with diverse tastes and make it juicier.

Preparation Time: 10 minutes

Cooking Time: 15 minutes

Servings: 4

Ingredients:

- 4 chicken breasts, skinless & boneless
- ¼ teaspoon red pepper flakes, crushed
- ½ teaspoon onion powder
- 2 teaspoons dried basil
- 3 garlic cloves, minced
- 2 tablespoons fresh lemon juice
- 123 g (½ cup) Greek yogurt
- Pepper
- Salt

Directions:

- In a large bowl, mix together yogurt, lemon juice, garlic, basil, onion powder, red pepper flakes, pepper, and salt.
- Add chicken and mix until well coated. Cover and place in refrigerator for 12 hours to marinate.
- Preheat the air fryer to 375 F/ 190 C.
- Remove chicken from refrigerator.
- Spray air fryer basket with cooking spray.

- Place marinated chicken into the air fryer basket and cook for 10 minutes.
- Flip chicken and cook for 5 minutes or until cooked.
- Serve and enjoy.

Nutritional Value (Amount per Serving):

- Calories 303, Fat 11.4 g, Carbohydrates 2.2 g, Sugar 1.3 g, Protein 45 g, Cholesterol 131 mg

5-Spicy Chicken Meatballs

Spicy chicken meatballs are a mouthwatering culinary creation that takes the humble ground chicken and elevates it to a whole new level of taste and excitement.

Preparation Time: 05 minutes

Cooking Time: 14 minutes

Servings: 8

Ingredients:

- 1 egg
- 680 g (1 ½ pounds) ground chicken
- ½ teaspoon garlic, minced
- 78 g (1/3 cup) cheddar cheese, shredded
- ½ onion, chopped
- 1/3 cup parsley, minced
- 2 jalapeno pepper, seeded & minced
- Pepper
- Salt

Directions:

- Preheat the air fryer to 390 F/ 193 C.
- In a bowl, mix together chicken and remaining ingredients until well combined.
- Spray air fryer basket with cooking spray.

- Make equal shapes of meatballs from the chicken mixture and place into the air fryer basket and cook for 12-14 minutes.
- Serve and enjoy.

Nutritional Value (Amount per Serving):

- Calories 193, Fat 8.5 g, Carbohydrates 1.2 g, Sugar 0.5 g, Protein 26.7 g, Cholesterol 101 mg

6-Perfect Chicken Patties

Perfect chicken patties are savory and delicious patties made from ground chicken and a variety of flavorful seasonings.

Preparation Time: 10 minutes

Cooking Time: 10 minutes

Servings: 8

Ingredients:

- 1 egg, lightly beaten
- 453 g (1 pound) ground chicken
- 48 g (½ cup) almond flour
- 2 tablespoons fresh herbs, chopped
- 1 zucchini, grated & squeeze out excess liquid
- 1 carrot, grated
- 1 medium onion, diced
- 2 teaspoons olive oil
- Pepper
- Salt

Directions:

- Heat oil in a pan over medium heat.
- Add onion to the pan and sauté until softened.
- Transfer sautéed onion to the mixing bowl.

- Add chicken and remaining ingredients into the bowl and mix until well combined.
- Make equal shapes of patties from the chicken mixture and place into the air fryer basket.
- Cook at 390 F/ 193 C for 10 minutes or until cooked. Flip patties halfway through.
- Serve and enjoy.

Nutritional Value (Amount per Serving):

- Calories 149, Fat 6.9 g, Carbohydrates 3.5 g, Sugar 1.5 g, Protein 18 g, Cholesterol 71 mg

7-Juicy Turkey Breast

A delightful turkey breast is a wonderful addition to your festive feast or any special gathering. By using the right cooking methods and flavors, you can savor tender, flavorful turkey meat that's sure to satisfy your guests.

Preparation Time: 10 minutes

Cooking Time: 60 minutes

Servings: 8

Ingredients:

- 900 g (2 pounds) turkey breast, bone-in & skin-on
- 1/2 teaspoon fresh thyme, chopped
- 1 tablespoon olive oil
- 1/2 teaspoon fresh sage, chopped
- 1/4 teaspoon pepper
- 1 teaspoon salt

Directions:

- In a small bowl, mix together oil, sage, thyme, pepper, and salt and rub all over the turkey breast.
- Place turkey breast into the air fryer basket and cook at 325 F/ 162 C for 30 minutes.
- Turn the turkey breast and cook for 30 minutes more or until the internal temperature of the turkey breast reaches 165 F.
- Slice and serve.

Nutritional Value (Amount per Serving):

- Calories 133, Fat 3.6 g, Carbohydrates 4.9 g, Sugar 4 g, Protein 19.4 g, Cholesterol 49 mg

8-Flavors Chicken Wings

Tasty chicken wings are small pieces of chicken that are made extra delicious by adding different flavors and spices to them.

Preparation Time: 10 minutes

Cooking Time: 25 minutes

Servings: 2

Ingredients:

- 453 g (1 pound) chicken wings
- 1 cup green curry sauce
- 2 teaspoons Thai curry seasoning
- 1 tablespoon potato starch
- 1 tablespoon basil, chopped
- 1 tablespoon fresh parsley, chopped

Directions:

- In a bowl, toss chicken wings with potato starch and curry seasoning.

- Add chicken wings into the air fryer basket and cook at 350 F/ 176 C for 30 minutes. Flip chicken wings after every 10 minutes.
- In a mixing bowl, mix together green curry sauce, parsley, and basil.
- Add cooked chicken wings and toss well to coat.
- Serve and enjoy.

Nutritional Value (Amount per Serving):

- Calories 522, Fat 21.6 g, Carbohydrates 10.1 g, Sugar 4.8 g, Protein 66.1 g, Cholesterol 202 mg

9-Easy Turkey Meatballs

Tasty chicken wings are little chunks of chicken that are made more delicious by adding different tastes and spices to them.

Preparation Time: 10 minutes

Cooking Time: 10 minutes

Servings: 4

Ingredients:

- 1 egg, lightly beaten
- 680 g (1 1/2 pounds) ground turkey
- 1/4 cup fresh parsley, minced
- 1 teaspoon paprika
- 1 bell pepper, chopped
- Pepper
- Salt

Directions:

- Preheat the air fryer to 400 F/ 204 C.
- In a bowl, mix together ground turkey, egg, parsley, paprika, bell pepper, salt, and pepper until well combined.

- Make equal shapes of balls from the meat mixture and place them into the air fryer basket.
- Cook meatballs for 8-10 minutes. Turn halfway through.
- Serve and enjoy.

Nutritional Value (Amount per Serving):

- Calories 360, Fat 19.9 g, Carbohydrates 2.9 g, Sugar 1.7 g, Protein 48.4 g, Cholesterol 214 mg

10-Turkey Patties

Turkey patties are savory and delicious patties made from ground turkey meat mixed with various seasonings and ingredients.

Preparation Time: 10 minutes

Cooking Time: 15 minutes

Servings: 5

Ingredients:

- 453 g (1 pound) ground turkey
- 1 tablespoon Worcestershire sauce
- 1/4 cup fresh cilantro, chopped
- 8 mushrooms, finely chopped
- 1 teaspoon onion powder
- 1 teaspoon garlic powder
- Pepper
- Salt

Directions:

- Add ground turkey and remaining ingredients into the bowl and mix until well combined.
- Make equal shapes of patties from the meat mixture.

- Spray the air fryer basket with cooking spray.
- Place patties into the air fryer basket and cook at 380 F/ 193 C for 15 minutes. Turn patties halfway through.
- Serve and enjoy.

Nutritional Value (Amount per Serving):

- Calories 190, Fat 10.1 g, Carbohydrates 2.4 g, Sugar 1.4 g, Protein 25.9 g, Cholesterol 93 mg

BEEF RECIPES

1-Meatballs

Meatballs are small, seasoned, and cooked portions of ground meat, a popular dish in various global cuisines.

Preparation Time: 10 minutes

Cooking Time: 14 minutes

Servings: 4

Ingredients:

- 1 egg
- 453 g (1 pound) ground beef
- 25 g (1/4 cup) almond flour
- 1/2 onion, chopped
- ¼ teaspoon paprika
- 1 teaspoon garlic powder
- Pepper
- Salt

Directions:

- Preheat the air fryer to 390 F/ 198 C.
- In a bowl, mix together egg, meat, paprika, garlic powder, almond flour,

onion, salt, and black pepper and mix until well combined.

- Make equal shapes of balls from the meat mixture and place them into the air fryer basket and cook for 14 minutes. Turn meatballs halfway through.
- Serve and enjoy.

Nutritional Value (Amount per Serving):

- Calories 211, Fat 6.8 g, Carbohydrates 3.5 g, Sugar 1 g, Protein 29.6 g, Cholesterol 114 mg

2-Asian Steak Bites

Asian steak bites are small, tender steak pieces soaked in a delectable sauce infused with Asian flavors.

Preparation Time: 10 minutes

Cooking Time: 10 minutes

Servings: 4

Ingredients:

- 453 g (1 pound) rib-eye steak, cut into 1/2-inch pieces
- 2 teaspoon dark soy sauce
- 2 teaspoons light soy sauce
- 1 tablespoon lemon juice
- 1 tablespoon rice wine
- 1 tablespoon oyster sauce
- 3 garlic cloves, chopped
- 8 mushrooms, sliced
- 2 tablespoons ginger, grated
- 1 teaspoon cornstarch
- 1/4 teaspoon pepper

Directions:

- Add steak pieces and remaining ingredients into the large mixing bowl and mix until well coated. Cover and place in refrigerator for 1 hour to marinate.
- Remove steak pieces and mushrooms from the marinade and add to the air fryer basket.
- Cook at 380 F/ 193 C for 10 minutes. Stir halfway through.
- Serve and enjoy.

Nutritional Value (Amount per Serving):

- Calories 346, Fat 25.4 g, Carbohydrates 8.7 g, Sugar 3.5 g, Protein 21.8 g, Cholesterol 75 mg

3-Marinated Sirloin Steak

Marinated sirloin steak is a flavorful and tender cut of beef that has been soaked in a seasoned mixture to enhance its taste and texture.

Preparation Time: 10 minutes

Cooking Time: 10 minutes

Servings: 4

Ingredients:

- 4 sirloin steak
- 1 tablespoon fresh thyme, chopped
- 2 tablespoons olive oil
- 2 tablespoon steak sauce
- 1/2 teaspoon coriander powder
- 2 garlic cloves, minced
- Pepper
- Salt

Directions:

- In a bowl, add steak and remaining ingredients and mix well to coat. Cover and set aside for 40 minutes.
- Preheat the air fryer to 360 F/ 182 C.
- Place marinated steak into the air fryer basket and cook for 8-10 minutes or until cooked.
- Serve and enjoy.

Nutritional Value (Amount per Serving):

- Calories 232, Fat 12.4 g, Carbohydrates 2.2 g, Sugar 1 g, Protein 25.9 g, Cholesterol 76 mg

4-Juicy Flank Steak

Juicy flank steak, a tender and flavorful beef cut, is often marinated or seasoned before cooking to enhance its taste and juiciness.

Preparation Time: 10 minutes

Cooking Time: 10 minutes

Servings: 4

Ingredients:

- 4 flank steak
- 1 tablespoon Worcestershire sauce
- 1 tablespoon soy sauce, low-sodium
- 1/4 cup red wine vinegar
- 1/4 cup olive oil
- 1 teaspoon garlic, minced
- 1 tablespoon Dijon mustard
- Pepper
- Salt

Directions:

- Add steak and remaining ingredients into the large mixing bowl and mix well. Cover and set aside for 40 minutes.

- Preheat the air fryer to 360 F/ 182 C.
- Place marinated steak into the air fryer basket and cook for 8-10 minutes or until cooked.
- Serve and enjoy.

Nutritional Value (Amount per Serving):

- Calories 288, Fat 19 g, Carbohydrates 1.7 g, Sugar 0.9 g, Protein 24.1 g, Cholesterol 47 mg

5-Quick & Easy Meatloaf

This quick and easy meatloaf recipe is a classic comfort meal ideal for busy weeknights or those seeking a hearty and delicious dinner.

Preparation Time: 10 minutes

Cooking Time: 20 minutes

Servings: 6

Ingredients:

- 2 eggs, lightly beaten
- 680 g (1 1/2 pounds) ground beef
- 1 tablespoon Worcestershire sauce
- 1 garlic clove, minced
- 1/4 cup unsweetened coconut milk
- 1 tablespoon steak seasoning
- 1/2 medium onion, grated
- 50 g (1/2 cup) almond flour
- 2 tablespoon bourbon
- Pepper
- Salt

Directions:

- Preheat the air fryer to 350 F/ 176 C.
- Grease the air fryer loaf pan with butter and set aside.

- In a bowl, add ground beef and remaining ingredients and mix until well combined.
- Transfer the meat mixture to the loaf pan.
- Place the loaf pan into the air fryer basket and cook for 20 minutes or until the toothpick comes out clean.
- Slice and serve.

Nutritional Value (Amount per Serving):

- Calories 293, Fat 9.2 g, Carbohydrates 8.6 g, Sugar 2 g, Protein 37.9 g, Cholesterol 157 mg

6-Asian Beef

Delicious Asian beef refers to dishes primarily containing beef, prepared using traditional Asian cuisine flavors and techniques.

Preparation Time: 10 minutes

Cooking Time: 20 minutes

Servings: 4

Ingredients:

- 453 g (1 pound) beef flank
- 1 1/2 tablespoons ginger garlic paste
- 1 tablespoon coconut sugar
- 3 tablespoons olive oil
- 2 tablespoons sesame oil
- 1/2 cup soy sauce, low-sodium
- Pepper

Directions:

- Add meat and remaining ingredients into the large mixing bowl and mix well. Cover and place in refrigerator for 2-3 hours to marinate.
- Remove meat from marinade and place into the air fryer basket.

- Cook at 350 F/ 176 C for 20 minutes or until cooked. Flip the meat halfway through.
- Serve and enjoy.

Nutritional Value (Amount per Serving):

- Calories 406, Fat 26.8 g, Carbohydrates 6.3 g, Sugar 2.8 g, Protein 33.8 g, Cholesterol 62 mg

7-Beef Skewers

Beef skewers, also known as beef kebabs, are a popular and delicious dish made by threading marinated beef pieces onto skewers and grilling or cooking them.

Preparation Time: 10 minutes

Cooking Time: 10 minutes

Servings: 4

Ingredients:

- 453 g (1 pound) beef ribs, cut into 1-inch pieces
- 1 bell pepper, cut into pieces
- 2 tablespoons soy sauce, low-sodium
- 1/2 onion, cut into pieces
- ½ teaspoon paprika
- 1/3 cup sour cream
- Pepper
- Salt

Directions:

- Preheat the air fryer to 400 F/ 204 C.
- In a bowl, mix meat, bell pepper, onion, soy sauce, paprika, sour cream, pepper, and salt. Cover and place in refrigerator for 2 hours to marinate.

- Thread marinated meat, onion, and bell pepper pieces onto the skewers.
- Place skewers in the air fryer basket and cook for 10 minutes. Flip skewers halfway through.
- Serve and enjoy.

Nutritional Value (Amount per Serving):

- Calories 215, Fat 8.9 g, Carbohydrates 4 g, Sugar 1.8 g, Protein 28.8 g, Cholesterol 88 mg

8-Marinated Beef Skewers

Marinated beef skewers are a delightful and satisfying dish ideal for outdoor barbecues, picnics, or as a flavorful main course.

Preparation Time: 10 minutes

Cooking Time: 8 minutes

Servings: 4

Ingredients:

- 680 g (1 1/2 pounds) sirloin steak, cut into 1-inch chunks
- 1 bell pepper, cut into pieces
- ½ teaspoon ground cumin
- ½ teaspoon paprika
- ½ teaspoon chili powder
- 1 onion, cut into pieces
- ¼ cup olive oil
- 1 tablespoon fresh lime juice
- 1 teaspoon garlic, minced
- Pepper
- Salt

Directions:

- Add meat pieces and remaining ingredients into the large mixing bowl

- and mix well to coat. Cover bowl and place in refrigerator for overnight.
- Preheat the air fryer to 400 F/ 204 C.
- Thread marinated steak pieces onto the skewers.
- Place meat skewers into the air fryer basket and cook for 8 minutes or until cooked. Turn skewers halfway through.
- Serve and enjoy.

Nutritional Value (Amount per Serving):

- Calories 466, Fat 24.5 g, Carbohydrates 5 g, Sugar 2.8 g, Protein 52.4 g, Cholesterol 152 mg

9-Tasty Steak Bites

Tasty steak bites are a delicious dish made from bite-sized pieces of tender steak, seasoned and cooked to perfection. They're perfect as an appetizer, snack, or main course.

Preparation Time: 10 minutes

Cooking Time: 20 minutes

Servings: 4

Ingredients:

- 453 g (1 pound) steaks, cut into 1/2-inch pieces
- 2 tablespoons olive oil
- 225 g (½ pound) potatoes, cut into 1/2-inch pieces
- ½ teaspoon garlic powder
- ½ teaspoon paprika
- 1 teaspoon Worcestershire sauce
- Pepper
- Salt

Directions:

- Add potatoes into the boiling water and cook for 5 minutes. Drain well.
- Preheat the air fryer to 400 F/ 204.
- In a bowl, toss steak and potatoes with remaining ingredients until well coated.
- Add steak and potato mixture into the air fryer basket and cook for 15 minutes or until cooked. Stir halfway through.
- Serve and enjoy.

Nutritional Value (Amount per Serving):

- Calories 316, Fat 11.5 g, Carbohydrates 9.4 g, Sugar 1 g, Protein 42 g, Cholesterol 117 mg

10-Spicy Steak

Spicy steak is a flavorful dish where a steak is seasoned and prepared with ingredients that add heat and spiciness to the meat.

Preparation Time: 10 minutes

Cooking Time: 15 minutes

Servings: 4

Ingredients:

- 453 g (1 pound) sirloin steaks
- 1/2 teaspoon cardamom powder
- 1 teaspoon ground cinnamon
- 1 teaspoon garam masala
- 1/2 teaspoon cayenne
- 1 teaspoon ground fennel
- 1 tablespoon ginger garlic paste
- ½ medium onion paste
- Pepper
- Salt

Directions:

- Add meat and remaining ingredients into the mixing bowl and mix well. Cover and place in refrigerator for overnight.
- Place marinated meat into the air fryer basket and cook at 330 F/ 165 C for 15 minutes. Flip the steak halfway through.
- Serve and enjoy.

Nutritional Value (Amount per Serving):

- Calories 246, Fat 10.6 g, Carbohydrates 4 g, Sugar 0.7 g, Protein 32.7 g, Cholesterol 104 mg

PORK RECIPES

1- Flavors Pork Tenderloin

Flavoring pork tenderloin enhances its taste and creates a delicious and pleasant dish, it is the perfect choice for special occasions or a tasty dinner.

Preparation Time: 10 minutes

Cooking Time: 15 minutes

Servings: 4

Ingredients:

- 900 g (2 pounds) pork tenderloins
- 1 teaspoon garlic, minced
- 1/2 teaspoon paprika
- 1/4 teaspoon cinnamon
- 1/2 teaspoon cayenne pepper
- 1/4 cup olive oil
- 1 teaspoon ground ginger
- 1/4 teaspoon ground coriander
- 1 tablespoon chili powder
- 1 teaspoon ground cumin
- Pepper
- Salt

Directions:

- In a small bowl, mix together cumin, chili powder, coriander, ginger, cayenne, cinnamon, paprika, garlic, pepper, and salt.
- Brush pork tenderloins with olive oil and rub with spice mixture.
- Place pork tenderloins into the air fryer basket.
- Cook at 360 F/ 182 C for 15 minutes.
- Slice and serve.

Nutritional Value (Amount per Serving):

- Calories 592, Fat 33 g, Carbohydrates 2.5 g, Sugar 0.2 g, Protein 68.3 g, Cholesterol 213 mg

2- Tender & Juicy Pork Tenderloin

Flavoring pork tenderloin is an excellent approach to improve its flavor and produce a delectable dish. It's ideal for special events or a delicious meal.

Preparation Time: 10 minutes

Cooking Time: 25 minutes

Servings: 4

Ingredients:

- 680 g (1 1/2 pounds) pork tenderloin
- 1 tablespoon olive oil
- 1/4 teaspoon fennel seeds, crushed
- 1 teaspoon dried thyme
- 1 teaspoon garlic, minced
- Pepper
- Salt

Directions:

- Add pork tenderloin and remaining ingredients into the large mixing bowl and mix until meat is well coated. Cover and place in refrigerator for overnight.
- Place marinated pork tenderloin into the air fryer basket.
- Cook at 350 F/ 176 C for 25 minutes. Turn tenderloin after 15 minutes.
- Slice and serve.

Nutritional Value (Amount per Serving):

- Calories 275, Fat 9.5 g, Carbohydrates 0.8 g, Sugar 0 g, Protein 44.7 g, Cholesterol 124 mg

3-Meatballs

Meatballs are indeed known for their delicious and savory flavor. They're a favorite comfort food in many cultures around the world due to their versatility and ability to be customized with various seasonings and ingredients.

Preparation Time: 10 minutes

Cooking Time: 10 minutes

Servings: 12

Ingredients:

- 2 eggs
- 900 g (2 pounds) ground pork
- 1 teaspoon sesame oil
- 1 teaspoon ginger garlic paste
- 1/3 teaspoon red pepper flakes, crushed
- 1 tablespoon green onion, chopped
- 1 teaspoon soy sauce, low-sodium
- ¼ teaspoon paprika
- 50 g (1/2 cup) almond flour
- Pepper
- Salt

Directions:

- Add meat and remaining ingredients into the bowl and mix until well combined.
- Make equal shapes of balls from the meat mixture and place them into the air fryer basket.
- Cook at 400 F/ 204 C for 10 minutes. Turn halfway through.
- Serve and enjoy.

Nutritional Value (Amount per Serving):

- Calories 143, Fat 4 g, Carbohydrates 3.6 g, Sugar 0.4 g, Protein 21.4 g, Cholesterol 82 mg

4- Dijon Pork Chops & Brussels Sprouts

Dijon Pork Chops and Brussels Sprouts is a delectable dish that combines tender pork chops with roasted Brussels sprouts in a creamy Dijon mustard sauce.

Preparation Time: 10 minutes

Cooking Time: 10 minutes

Servings: 2

Ingredients:

- 2 pork chops
- 1 teaspoon Dijon mustard
- 1 teaspoon maple syrup
- ¼ teaspoon garlic powder
- 75 g (6 oz) Brussels sprouts, quartered
- 1 teaspoon olive oil
- Pepper
- Salt

Directions:

- In a small bowl, mix oil, Dijon mustard, garlic powder, maple syrup, pepper, and salt.
- Brush pork chops with oil mixture and place into the air fryer basket.
- Add Brussels sprouts on top of pork chops.
- Cook at 400 F/ 204 C for 10 minutes.
- Serve and enjoy.

Nutritional Value (Amount per Serving):

- Calories 326, Fat 22 g, Carbohydrates 10.1 g, Sugar 3.8 g, Protein 21 g, Cholesterol 69 mg

5- Crispy Parmesan Pork Chops

Crispy Parmesan Pork Chops are a comforting and delicious dish that pairs well with mashed potatoes, steamed vegetables, or fresh salads due to their crispy coating and cheesy Parmesan flavor.

Preparation Time: 10 minutes

Cooking Time: 12 minutes

Servings: 6

Ingredients:

- 680 g (1 1/2 pounds) pork chops, boneless
- 1 teaspoon garlic powder
- 1/4 cup parmesan cheese, grated
- 1 teaspoon paprika
- 1 teaspoon Creole seasoning
- 30 g (1/3 cup) almond flour

Directions:

- Preheat the air fryer to 360 F/ 182 C.
- Add pork chops and remaining ingredients into the zip-lock bag. Seal the bag and shake well to coat the pork chops.
- Place coated pork chops into the air fryer basket and cook for 10-12 minutes or until cooked. Flip pork chops halfway through.
- Serve and enjoy.

Nutritional Value (Amount per Serving):

- Calories 386, Fat 29.8 g, Carbohydrates 1 g, Sugar 0.2 g, Protein 27.2 g, Cholesterol 100 mg

6-Easy & Quick Pork Chops

The Easy and Quick Pork Chops are an excellent choice for a weeknight dinner, that provides us flavorful and satisfying meal without spending too much time in the kitchen.

Preparation Time: 10 minutes

Cooking Time: 10 minutes

Servings: 2

Ingredients:

- 2 pork chops, boneless
- 1/4 teaspoon garlic powder
- 1/2 teaspoon lemon zest, grated
- 1/2 teaspoon smoked paprika
- 1 tablespoon olive oil
- 1/8 teaspoon red pepper flakes, crushed
- 1/4 teaspoon onion powder
- 3/4 teaspoon rosemary, chopped
- Pepper
- Salt

Directions:

- In a small bowl, mix garlic powder, onion powder, rosemary, paprika, lemon zest, red pepper flakes, pepper, and salt.
- Brush pork chops with oil and rub with spice mixture.
- Place pork chops into the air fryer basket.
- Cook at 390 F/ 198 C for 10 minutes. Turn halfway through.
- Serve and enjoy.

Nutritional Value (Amount per Serving):

- Calories 326, Fat 27 g, Carbohydrates 1.3 g, Sugar 0.3 g, Protein 18.2 g, Cholesterol 70 mg

- Calories 336, Fat 27.4 g, Carbohydrates 3.1 g, Sugar 0.2 g, Protein 18.5 g, Cholesterol 69 mg

7-Garlic Herb Pork Chops

Garlic Herb Pork Chops are a delectable and satisfying meal, bursting with the rich flavors of garlic and a blend of herbs.

Preparation Time: 10 minutes

Cooking Time: 15 minutes

Servings: 2

Ingredients:

- 2 pork chops, boneless
- 1/2 teaspoon red pepper flakes
- 1 teaspoon fennel seeds, crushed
- 1 teaspoon fresh sage, chopped
- 1 tablespoon olive oil
- 1 lemon zest, grated
- 1 teaspoon garlic, minced
- 2 teaspoons fresh rosemary, chopped
- Pepper
- Salt

Directions:

- In a small bowl, mix together oil, fennel seeds, sage, lemon zest, garlic, red pepper flakes, rosemary, pepper, and salt.
- Brush pork chops with oil mixture and place into the air fryer basket.
- Cook at 380 F/ 193 C for 15 minutes. Turn halfway through.
- Serve and enjoy.

Nutritional Value (Amount per Serving):

8-Balsamic Dijon Pork Chops

Balsamic Dijon Pork Chops are a delectable dish featuring tender pork chops seasoned with a flavorful balsamic vinegar and Dijon mustard sauce.

Preparation Time: 10 minutes

Cooking Time: 12 minutes

Servings: 2

Ingredients:

- 453 g (1 pound) pork chops, boneless
- 1 tablespoon Dijon mustard
- 1 teaspoon olive oil
- ¼ teaspoon paprika
- 1 tablespoon balsamic vinegar
- Pepper
- Salt

Directions:

- In a small bowl, mix together oil, balsamic vinegar, paprika, Dijon mustard, pepper, and salt.
- Brush pork chops with oil mixture and place into the air fryer basket.
- Cook at 400 F/ 204 C for 12 minutes. Turn halfway through.
- Serve and enjoy.

Nutritional Value (Amount per Serving):

- Calories 756, Fat 59 g, Carbohydrates 0.5 g, Sugar 0.1 g, Protein 51.3 g, Cholesterol 195 mg

9-Crispy Crusted Pork Chops

Crispy Crusted Pork Chops are a delicious meal that combines tender pork chops with a golden, crunchy coating, known for their irresistible texture and savory flavor.

Preparation Time: 10 minutes

Cooking Time: 14 minutes

Servings: 4

Ingredients:

- 1 egg, lightly beaten
- 4 pork chops, boneless
- 50 g (1/2 cup) almond flour
- 45 g (1/2 cup) parmesan cheese, grated
- ¼ teaspoon garlic powder
- ¼ teaspoon paprika
- Pepper
- Salt

Directions:

- Add eggs into the shallow bowl and whisk well.
- In a separate shallow bowl, mix together parmesan cheese, garlic powder, paprika, almond flour, pepper, and salt.
- Dip each pork chop in egg then coat with cheese mixture.
- Place coated pork chops into the air fryer basket and cook at 360 F/ 182 C for 14 minutes. Turn halfway through.
- Serve and enjoy.

Nutritional Value (Amount per Serving):

- Calories 326, Fat 25.1 g, Carbohydrates 1.2 g, Sugar 0.2 g, Protein 23.7 g, Cholesterol 118 mg

10-Marinated Pork Skewers

Marinated Pork Skewers are a flavorful and versatile dish that's perfect for summer barbecues or a quick and satisfying meal any time of the year.

Preparation Time: 10 minutes

Cooking Time: 10 minutes

Servings: 4

Ingredients:

- 453 g (1 pound) pork shoulder, cut into 1/2-inch cubes
- 2 tablespoons sweet chili sauce
- 2 tablespoons brown sugar
- 1 tablespoon fish sauce
- 1 tablespoon garlic, minced
- 1 tablespoon sesame oil
- 1/4 cup soy sauce, low-sodium

Directions:

- Add meat and remaining ingredients into the large mixing bowl and mix well. Cover and place in refrigerator for overnight.
- Thread marinated meat onto the soaked skewers.
- Place skewers into the air fryer basket and cook at 380 F/ 193 C for 8-10 minutes. Turn halfway through.
- Serve and enjoy.

Nutritional Value (Amount per Serving):

- Calories 402, Fat 27.7 g, Carbohydrates 10 g, Sugar 7.8 g, Protein 27.8 g, Cholesterol 102 mg

LAMB RECIPES

1-Flavorful Lamb Shoulder

Lamb's rich and distinctive flavor pairs well with a wide range of seasonings and ingredients, making it a versatile choice for a variety of cuisines and cooking methods.

Preparation Time: 10 minutes

Cooking Time: 15 minutes

Servings: 6

Ingredients:

- 900 g (2 pounds) lamb shoulder, boneless
- 1 teaspoon ground fennel
- 1 tablespoon sesame seeds
- 1 tablespoon chili powder
- 2 tablespoons cumin powder
- 1 teaspoon cumin seeds
- 1 teaspoon garlic powder
- 1 teaspoon ground ginger
- Pepper
- Salt

Directions:

- In a small bowl, mix together fennel, sesame seeds, chili powder, cumin powder, cumin seeds, garlic powder, ginger, pepper, and salt and rub all over lamb shoulder.
- Place lamb shoulder into the air fryer basket.
- Cook at 350 F/ 176 C for 10-15 minutes.
- Slice and serve.

Nutritional Value (Amount per Serving):

- Calories 266, Fat 10.8 g, Carbohydrates 2.6 g, Sugar 0.3 g, Protein 37.2 g, Cholesterol 117 mg

2-Herb Lemon Lamb Chops

These Herb Lemon Lamb Chops are a delightful combination of savory herbs and zesty lemon that perfectly complement the tender lamb.

Preparation Time: 10 minutes

Cooking Time: 6 minutes

Servings: 8

Ingredients:

- 8 lamb chops
- 1/4 cup olive oil
- 1 tablespoon thyme, chopped
- 1 teaspoon garlic, minced
- 1 lemon zest, grated
- 1 tablespoon rosemary, chopped
- 1/2 teaspoon dried oregano
- 2 tablespoons fresh lemon juice
- Pepper
- Salt

Directions:

- Add lamb chops and remaining ingredients into the large mixing bowl and mix well. Cover and place in refrigerator for 1 hour.
- Place lamb chops into the air fryer basket.
- Cook at 400 F/ 204 C for 6 minutes.
- Serve and enjoy.

Nutritional Value (Amount per Serving):

- Calories 215, Fat 12.7 g, Carbohydrates 1 g, Sugar 0.1 g, Protein 24 g, Cholesterol 77 mg

- Calories 275, Fat 13 g, Carbohydrates 0.7 g, Sugar 0.1 g, Protein 37.4 g, Cholesterol 156 mg

3-Easy Lamb Kebabs

Easy Lamb Kebabs are a quick and delicious way to enjoy the rich, savory flavor of lamb. Aromatic spices make the tender, grilled meat even more delicious.

Preparation Time: 10 minutes

Cooking Time: 20 minutes

Servings: 4

Ingredients:

- 1 egg, lightly beaten
- 510 g (18 oz) ground lamb
- 1 teaspoon ground cumin
- 1 teaspoon chili powder
- 2 teaspoons olive oil
- ½ teaspoon paprika
- 1 teaspoon ginger garlic paste
- Pepper
- Salt

Directions:

- Preheat the air fryer to 390 F/ 198 C.
- Add ground lamb and remaining ingredients into the mixing bowl and mix until well combined.
- Make four sausage shape kebabs from the meat mixture.
- Place prepared kebabs into the air fryer basket and cook for 20 minutes. Flip halfway through.
- Serve and enjoy.

Nutritional Value (Amount per Serving):

4-Quick Lamb Chops

Quick Lamb Chops offers a quick and easy way to enjoy the delicious taste of lamb. The tender meat's richness is enhanced by the blend of garlic and aromatic herbs, making it a hassle-free and flavorful choice.

Preparation Time: 10 minutes

Cooking Time: 10 minutes

Servings: 4

Ingredients:

- 453 g (1 pound) lamb chops
- 1 teaspoon ground coriander
- 1 teaspoon oregano
- 2 tablespoons fresh lemon juice
- 2 tablespoons olive oil
- 1 teaspoon thyme
- 1 teaspoon rosemary
- Salt

Directions:

- Add lamb chops and remaining ingredients into the large mixing bowl and mix until well coated. Cover bowl and place in refrigerator for 2-3 hours to marinate lamb chops.
- Remove lamb chops from marinade and place into the air fryer basket.
- Cook at 400 F/ 204 C for 10 minutes.
- Serve and enjoy.

Nutritional Value (Amount per Serving):

- Calories 274, Fat 15 g, Carbohydrates 0.8 g, Sugar 0.2 g, Protein 32 g, Cholesterol 102 mg

5-Tasty Lamb Skewers

Tasty Lamb Skewers are a delicious treat made by threading marinated lamb pieces onto skewers and grilling them to perfection.

Preparation Time: 10 minutes

Cooking Time: 10 minutes

Servings: 4

Ingredients:

- 453 g (1 pound) lamb shoulder chops, cut into 1-inch pieces
- 2 teaspoons granulated garlic
- 1 teaspoon fennel seed, crushed
- 2 teaspoons dry sherry
- 1 tablespoon olive oil
- 1 tablespoon ground cumin
- 1 tablespoon red chili flakes, crushed
- Pepper
- Salt

Directions:

- Add meat and remaining ingredients into the bowl and mix until meat is well coated. Cover and set aside for 20 minutes.
- Preheat the air fryer to 340 F/ 171 C.
- Thread marinated meat pieces onto the skewers.
- Place meat skewers into the air fryer basket and cook for 10-12 minutes or until cooked. Turn halfway through.
- Serve and enjoy.

Nutritional Value (Amount per Serving):

- Calories 222, Fat 12 g, Carbohydrates 2 g, Sugar 0.4 g, Protein 22.7 g, Cholesterol 75 mg

6-Garlic Mint Lamb Chops

Garlic Mint Lamb Chops are a delicious meal showcasing succulent lamb chops seasoned with garlic and fresh mint for a burst of flavor.

Preparation Time: 10 minutes

Cooking Time: 15 minutes

Servings: 4

Ingredients:

- 12 lamb loin chops
- 1/2 cup olive oil
- 3 fresh lime juice
- 1 tablespoon lime zest
- 2 tablespoons garlic, minced
- 1/4 cup fresh mint, chopped
- Pepper
- Salt

Directions:

- Add lamb chops and remaining ingredients into the large mixing bowl and mix well. Cover and place in refrigerator for 3-4 hours.
- Remove lamb chops from marinade and place into the air fryer basket.
- Cook at 370 F/ 187 C for 15 minutes. Turn halfway through.
- Serve and enjoy.

Nutritional Value (Amount per Serving):

- Calories 713, Fat 44 g, Carbohydrates 5.5 g, Sugar 0.7 g, Protein 72.3 g, Cholesterol 230 mg

7-Juicy Lamb Chops

Juicy Lamb Chops are a delectable dish featuring succulent lamb chops cooked to perfection, ensuring they are tender and flavorful.

Preparation Time: 10 minutes

Cooking Time: 15 minutes

Servings: 4

Ingredients:

- 8 loin lamb chops
- 1/2 teaspoon olive oil
- 2 tablespoons mustard
- 1 tablespoon fresh lemon juice
- 1 teaspoon tarragon
- Pepper
- Salt

Directions:

- Preheat the air fryer to 390 F/ 198 C.
- Add lamb chops and remaining ingredients into the large mixing bowl and mix well. Cover and place in refrigerator for 40 minutes.
- Place marinated lamb chops into the air fryer basket and cook for 15 minutes or until cooked. Turn halfway through.
- Serve and enjoy.

Nutritional Value (Amount per Serving):

- Calories 676, Fat 54.2 g, Carbohydrates 2.1 g, Sugar 0.5 g, Protein 39.5 g, Cholesterol 160 mg

8-Meatballs

Meatballs, a popular and hearty dish globally enjoyed, can be customized with herbs, spices, and grated vegetables, making them a versatile and delicious choice.

Preparation Time: 10 minutes

Cooking Time: 15 minutes

Servings: 6

Ingredients:

- 453 g (1 pound) ground lamb
- 1/2 teaspoon turmeric
- 60 g (1/3 cup) zucchini, grated
- 15 g (1/2 cup) parsley, chopped
- 1 teaspoon garlic, minced
- 1/2 teaspoon coriander
- 1/2 teaspoon cumin
- 1 small onion, chopped
- 1 bell pepper, chopped
- Pepper
- Salt

Directions:

- Add meat and remaining ingredients into the bowl and mix until well combined.
- Make equal shapes of balls from the meat mixture and place them into the air fryer basket.
- Cook at 370 F/ 187 C for 15 minutes. Turn halfway through.
- Serve and enjoy.

Nutritional Value (Amount per Serving):

- Calories 156, Fat 5.7 g, Carbohydrates 2.9 g, Sugar 1.4 g, Protein 21.7 g, Cholesterol 68 mg

9-Easy Balsamic Lamb Chops

Balsamic lamb chops are a delectable and easy-to-prepare dish perfect for special occasions or weeknight dinners, offering a flavorful and elegant meal.

Preparation Time: 10 minutes

Cooking Time: 15 minutes

Servings: 4

Ingredients:

- 4 lamb chops
- 1 teaspoon garlic, crushed
- 2 tablespoons olive oil
- 1/4 cup balsamic vinegar
- 1/2 teaspoon onion powder
- 1/2 teaspoon smoked paprika
- Pepper
- Salt

Directions:

- Preheat the air fryer to 400 F/ 204 C.
- Add lamb chops and remaining ingredients into the large mixing bowl and mix well. Cover and place in refrigerator for 50 minutes to marinate.
- Place lamb chops into the air fryer basket and cook for 15 minutes or until cooked. Turn halfway through.
- Serve and enjoy.

Nutritional Value (Amount per Serving):

- Calories 228, Fat 13.3 g, Carbohydrates 0.8 g, Sugar 0.2 g, Protein 24 g, Cholesterol 77 mg

10-Delicious Lamb Kofta

Lamb kofta is a Middle Eastern and Mediterranean food made from spicy ground lamb. These patties are grilled or pan-fried and

given with different sides like pita bread, rice, and salad.

Preparation Time: 10 minutes

Cooking Time: 12 minutes

Servings: 6

Ingredients:

- 900 g (2 pounds) ground lamb
- 1/2 teaspoon cinnamon
- 1 teaspoon paprika
- 1 tablespoon ground cumin
- 1 tablespoon ground coriander
- 2 tablespoons fresh parsley, chopped
- 1 teaspoon garlic, minced
- Pepper
- Salt

Directions:

- Add ground lamb and remaining ingredients into the mixing bowl and mix until well combined.
- Make 4-inch long logs from the meat mixture and place into the air fryer basket.
- Cook at 400 F/ 204 C for 12 minutes or until cooked.
- Serve and enjoy.

Nutritional Value (Amount per Serving):

- Calories 292, Fat 11.4 g, Carbohydrates 1.2 g, Sugar 0.1 g, Protein 42.8 g, Cholesterol 136 mg

FISH AND SEAFOOD RECIPES

1-Salmon Patties

Salmon patties are protein-rich dishes made from canned or fresh salmon, mixed with various ingredients, and pan-fried until get a crispy result.

Preparation Time: 10 minutes

Cooking Time: 12 minutes

Servings: 3

Ingredients:

- 1 egg
- 340 g (12 oz) can salmon, drained
- 2 teaspoons arrowroot starch
- 2 tablespoons green onion, chopped
- ½ teaspoon garlic, minced
- 1 teaspoon dried dill
- 1 tablespoon fresh lemon juice
- Pepper
- Salt

Directions:

- Add salmon and remaining ingredients into the mixing bowl and mix until well combined.
- Make equal shapes of patties from the salmon mixture and place into the air fryer basket.
- Cook at 400 F/ 204 C for 12 minutes. Turn halfway through.
- Serve and enjoy.

Nutritional Value (Amount per Serving):

- Calories 167, Fat 7.4 g, Carbohydrates 2 g, Sugar 0.2 g, Protein 21.4 g, Cholesterol 78 mg

2-Greek Salmon Fillets

Greek salmon fillets are a delectable and flavorful dish infused with Mediterranean-inspired flavors and ingredients.

Preparation Time: 10 minutes

Cooking Time: 10 minutes

Servings: 2

Ingredients:

- 2 salmon fillets
- 70 g (1/2 cup) marinated tomatoes
- 1 teaspoon Greek seasoning
- 45 g (1/4 cup) olives, sliced
- 1 oz feta cheese, crumbled
- 1 teaspoon olive oil
- Pepper
- Salt

Directions:

- Brush fish fillets with oil and season with Greek seasoning, pepper, and salt.
- Place fish fillets into the air fryer basket.
- Cook at 360 F/ 182 C for 10 minutes.
- Place cooked fish fillets on a plate and top with tomatoes, feta cheese, and olives.
- Serve and enjoy.

Nutritional Value (Amount per Serving):

- Calories 354, Fat 21.3 g, Carbohydrates 3.1 g, Sugar 0.8 g, Protein 39.3 g, Cholesterol 93 mg

3-Salmon with Veggies

Salmon with vegetables is a nutritious and delicious dish that pairs tender salmon fillets with a variety of vegetables, making it easy to prepare and enjoy.

Preparation Time: 10 minutes

Cooking Time: 10 minutes

Servings: 2

Ingredients:

- 2 salmon fillets
- 1 tablespoon olive oil
- 90 g (1/2 cup) roasted red peppers, sliced
- 110 g (1 cup) mushrooms, sliced
- 1/2 teaspoon dill weed
- 1 tablespoon fresh lemon juice
- Pepper
- Salt

Directions:

- In a small bowl, mix oil, dill, lemon juice, pepper, and salt.
- Brush fish fillets with oil mixture and place into the air fryer basket.
- Add roasted peppers and mushrooms around the fish fillets and cook at 400 F/ 200 C for 10 minutes.
- Serve and enjoy.

Nutritional Value (Amount per Serving):

- Calories 306, Fat 17 g, Carbohydrates 4.3 g, Sugar 2.8 g, Protein 36.2 g, Cholesterol 94 mg

4- Quick Scallops

Quick scallops are a quick and delicious seafood dish ideal for busy weeknight dinners or special occasions, providing elegance without excessive kitchen time.

Preparation Time: 10 minutes

Cooking Time: 8 minutes

Servings: 4

Ingredients:

- 453 g (1 pound) scallops
- 1 lemon juice
- 1 tablespoon garlic, minced
- 1 tablespoon dill, chopped
- 1 tablespoon olive oil
- 2 tablespoons butter, melted
- Pepper
- Salt

Directions:

- In a bowl, toss scallops with lemon juice, dill, oil, garlic, butter, pepper, and salt.
- Add scallops into the air fryer basket.
- Cook at 400 F/ 204 C for 6-8 minutes. Stir halfway through.
- Serve and enjoy.

Nutritional Value (Amount per Serving):

- Calories 192, Fat 10.3 g, Carbohydrates 4.1 g, Sugar 0.3 g, Protein 19.5 g, Cholesterol 53 mg

5-Cheese Herb Shrimp

Cheese herb shrimp is a delicious seafood dish that combines succulent shrimp with a flavorful cheese and herb sauce.

Preparation Time: 10 minutes

Cooking Time: 10 minutes

Servings: 6

Ingredients:

- 900 g (2 pounds) cooked shrimp, peeled & deveined
- 1 teaspoon basil
- 1/2 teaspoon oregano
- 60 g (2/3 cup) parmesan cheese, grated
- 2 tablespoons olive oil
- 1 teaspoon onion powder
- 3 garlic cloves, minced
- Pepper
- Salt

Directions:

- In a bowl, toss shrimp with oil, onion powder, basil, oregano, cheese, garlic, pepper, and salt.
- Add shrimp mixture into the air fryer basket.
- Cook at 350 F/ 176 C for 8-10 minutes.
- Serve and enjoy.

Nutritional Value (Amount per Serving):

- Calories 258, Fat 9.4 g, Carbohydrates 3.5 g, Sugar 0.2 g, Protein 37.8 g, Cholesterol 326 mg

6-Tasty Shrimp Skewers

These delicious shrimp skewers are a quick and easy way to enjoy a flavorful meal, perfect for summer barbecues or a simple weeknight dinner.

Preparation Time: 10 minutes

Cooking Time: 10 minutes

Servings: 4

Ingredients:

- 453 g (1 pound) shrimp
- 2 garlic cloves, minced
- 1 tablespoon old bay seasoning

- 1 tablespoon olive oil
- 1 tablespoon lime juice
- Pepper
- Salt

Directions:

- Add shrimp and remaining ingredients into the bowl and toss until well coated.
- Thread shrimp onto the soaked skewers.
- Place shrimp skewers into the air fryer basket and cook at 390 F/ 198 C for 8-10 minutes.
- Serve and enjoy.

Nutritional Value (Amount per Serving):

- Calories 164, Fat 5.5 g, Carbohydrates 2 g, Sugar 0.1 g, Protein 25.9 g, Cholesterol 239 mg

7-Pesto Scallops

Pesto scallops are a delightful seafood dish that combines tender scallops with a vibrant and aromatic pesto sauce.

Preparation Time: 10 minutes

Cooking Time: 10 minutes

Servings: 4

Ingredients:

- 453 g(1 pound) sea scallops
- 2 garlic cloves, minced
- 3 tablespoons heavy cream
- 1 tablespoon olive oil
- 1/4 cup basil pesto
- Pepper
- Salt

Directions:

- In a small saucepan, add oil, pesto, garlic, heavy cream, pepper, and salt and simmer for 2-3 minutes. Remove saucepan from heat.
- Season scallops with pepper and salt and add to the air fryer basket.
- Cook at 320 F/ 160 C for 5 minutes. Flip scallops and cook for 3 minutes more.
- Pour sauce over scallops and serve.

Nutritional Value (Amount per Serving):

- Calories 174, Fat 8.5 g, Carbohydrates 3.5 g, Sugar 0 g, Protein 19.4 g, Cholesterol 53 mg

8-Asian Salmon

Asian salmon is a fragrant and savory dish that harmoniously blends salmon with key ingredients from Asian cuisine, including soy sauce, ginger, garlic, and sesame.

Preparation Time: 10 minutes

Cooking Time: 10 minutes

Servings: 4

Ingredients:

- 4 salmon fillets
- 1 tablespoon sesame oil
- 1 tablespoon sriracha
- 1/4 cup honey
- 1 tablespoon garlic, minced
- 2 tablespoons soy sauce, low-sodium
- Pepper
- Salt

Directions:

- In a bowl, coat fish fillets with oil, soy sauce, honey, sriracha, garlic, pepper, and

salt. Cover and place in refrigerator for 50 minutes.
- Preheat the air fryer to 375 F/ 190 C.
- Place marinated fish fillets into the air fryer basket and cook for 8-10 minutes or until cooked.
- Serve and enjoy.

Nutritional Value (Amount per Serving):

- Calories 345, Fat 14.4 g, Carbohydrates 19.5 g, Sugar 17.6 g, Protein 35.2 g, Cholesterol 78 mg

9- Lemon Pepper Fish Fillets

Lemon pepper fish fillets are a quick and easy way to enjoy citrus and spice with your favorite fish, making them a light and satisfying meal.

Preparation Time: 10 minutes

Cooking Time: 10 minutes

Servings: 4

Ingredients:

- 4 tilapia fillets
- 1 1/2 teaspoons ground peppercorns
- 2 tablespoons olive oil
- 1/8 teaspoon smoked paprika
- 1 teaspoon garlic, minced
- 2 tablespoons lemon zest, grated
- Salt

Directions:

- In a small bowl, mix together oil, peppercorns, paprika, garlic, lemon zest, and salt.
- Brush fish fillets with oil mixture and place into the air fryer basket.
- Cook at 400 F/ 204 C for 8-10 minutes.

- Serve and enjoy.

Nutritional Value (Amount per Serving):

- Calories 154, Fat 8 g, Carbohydrates 1.1 g, Sugar 0.2 g, Protein 21.2 g, Cholesterol 55 mg

10-Marinated Salmon with Veggies

Marinated salmon with veggies is a delicious and wholesome dish that combines succulent salmon fillets with a medley of roasted or grilled vegetables.

Preparation Time: 10 minutes

Cooking Time: 10 minutes

Servings: 4

Ingredients:

- 4 salmon fillets
- 2 tablespoons soy sauce, low-sodium
- 1/4 cup orange juice
- 2 tablespoons olive oil
- 1/4 cup mirin
- 1 zucchini, sliced
- 2 garlic cloves, minced
- 2 bell peppers, cut into 1-inch pieces
- 1 teaspoon ground ginger
- 1 tablespoon honey
- 1 tablespoon lemon juice
- 2 tomatoes, diced
- Pepper
- Salt

Directions:

- In a large mixing bowl, mix salmon with the remaining ingredients. Cover and place in refrigerator for 50 minutes.
- Preheat the air fryer to 360 F/ 182 C.
- Place marinated salmon and vegetables into the air fryer basket and cook for 10 minutes.
- Serve and enjoy.

Nutritional Value (Amount per Serving):

- Calories 392, Fat 18.4 g, Carbohydrates 22.7 g, Sugar 15.3 g, Protein 37 g, Cholesterol 78 mg

11-Curried Fish Fillets

Curried fish fillets are a delectable dish that combines tender fish fillets with a rich and fragrant curry sauce.

Preparation Time: 10 minutes

Cooking Time: 10 minutes

Servings: 2

Ingredients:

- 2 cod fillets
- 1/8 teaspoon smoked paprika
- 1/4 teaspoon curry powder
- 1 tablespoon olive oil
- 2 tablespoons basil, sliced
- 1/8 teaspoon garlic powder
- Pepper
- Salt

Directions:

- In a small bowl, mix oil, paprika, curry powder, garlic powder, pepper, and salt.
- Brush fish fillets with oil mixture and place into the air fryer basket.

- Cook at 360 F/ 182 C for 8-10 minutes.
- Garnish with basil and serve.

Nutritional Value (Amount per Serving):

- Calories 146, Fat 6.8 g, Carbohydrates 0.5 g, Sugar 0.1 g, Protein 20.2 g, Cholesterol 70 mg

12-Tuna Patties

Tuna patties, also known as tuna cakes or tuna burgers, are a tasty and budget-friendly dish made from canned tuna, breadcrumbs, and various seasonings.

Preparation Time: 10 minutes

Cooking Time: 10 minutes

Servings: 4

Ingredients:

- 1 egg, lightly beaten
- 370 g (2 cans) tuna, drained
- 2 tablespoons mayonnaise
- 25 g (1/4 cup) almond flour
- 1/4 cup can corn, drained
- 1/4 teaspoon dried basil
- 1/4 teaspoon garlic powder
- Pepper
- Salt

Directions:

- In a bowl, mix tuna with remaining ingredients until well combined.
- Make equal shapes of patties from the tuna mixture and place into the air fryer basket.
- Cook at 360 F/ 182 C for 8-10 minutes. Turn halfway through.
- Serve and enjoy.

Nutritional Value (Amount per Serving):

- Calories 248, Fat 11.2 g, Carbohydrates 8.8 g, Sugar 1.3 g, Protein 26.3 g, Cholesterol 70 mg

13-Spicy Prawns

Spicy prawns, a culinary delight, showcase the succulent and tender nature of prawns, elevated to new heights with the infusion of a fiery and richly aromatic spice blend.

Preparation Time: 10 minutes

Cooking Time: 7 minutes

Servings: 2

Ingredients:

- 15 fresh prawns
- 1 tablespoon sweet chili sauce
- 1 teaspoon chili powder
- 1 1/2 tablespoons olive oil
- 2 garlic cloves, minced
- Pepper
- Salt

Directions:

- Preheat the air fryer to 360 F/ 182 C.
- In a bowl, mix prawns, oil, chili powder, garlic, sweet chili sauce, pepper, and salt.
- Add prawns into the air fryer basket and cook for 5-7 minutes or until cooked.
- Serve and enjoy.

Nutritional Value (Amount per Serving):

- Calories 305, Fat 13.5 g, Carbohydrates 6.7 g, Sugar 3.1 g, Protein 37.9 g, Cholesterol 347 mg

14-Shrimp & Veggies

Shrimp and veggies is a visually appealing and nutritious dish that pairs succulent shrimp with a variety of colorful vegetables, providing a burst of flavor and essential nutrients.

Preparation Time: 10 minutes

Cooking Time: 8 minutes

Servings: 4

Ingredients:

- 340 g (12 oz) shrimp
- 100 g (1 cup) cauliflower, chopped
- 2 tablespoons olive oil
- 1 tablespoon garlic herb seasoning
- 1/2 fresh lemon juice
- 175 g (1 cup) broccoli, chopped
- Pepper
- Salt

Directions:

- Preheat the air fryer to 400 F.
- In a mixing bowl, toss shrimp, cauliflower, broccoli, lemon juice, oil, garlic herb seasoning, pepper, and salt.
- Add shrimp mixture into the air fryer basket and cook for 6 minutes.
- Stir well and cook for 2 minutes more.
- Serve and enjoy.

Nutritional Value (Amount per Serving):

- Calories 174, Fat 8.6 g, Carbohydrates 4.3 g, Sugar 1.1 g, Protein 20.6 g, Cholesterol 179 mg

15-Tasty Tuna Steaks

Tasty Tuna steaks are renowned for their savory and delicious taste, owing to their natural richness and meaty texture, making them a popular choice among seafood enthusiasts.

Preparation Time: 10 minutes

Cooking Time: 10 minutes

Servings: 2

Ingredients:

- 453 g (1 pound) tuna steaks
- 1 teaspoon thyme
- ¼ teaspoon paprika
- 1/4 cup olive oil
- 5 garlic cloves, minced
- Pepper
- Salt

Directions:

- In a bowl, coat tuna steaks with oil, garlic, paprika, thyme, pepper, and salt. Cover and set aside for 20 minutes.
- Place marinated tuna steaks into the air fryer basket.
- Cook at 400 F/ 204 C for 8-10 minutes or until cooked.
- Serve and enjoy.

Nutritional Value (Amount per Serving):

- Calories 667, Fat 39.6 g, Carbohydrates 6.4 g, Sugar 1.1 g, Protein 69.2 g, Cholesterol 111 mg

VEGETARIAN RECIPES

1-Chili Lime Brussels sprouts

Chili Lime Brussels Sprouts are a zesty side dish that blends the earthy flavor of Brussels sprouts with the heat of chili and the tanginess of lime.

Preparation Time: 10 minutes

Cooking Time: 20 minutes

Servings: 4

Ingredients:

- 453 g (1 pound) Brussels sprouts, cut in half
- 1 teaspoon olive oil
- 1 tablespoon garlic, minced
- 3 teaspoons lime juice
- 2 tablespoons sweet chili sauce
- Pepper
- Salt

Directions:

- In a bowl, toss Brussels sprouts with oil, pepper, garlic, and salt.
- Add Brussels sprouts into the air fryer basket and cook at 350 F/ 176 C for 18-20 minutes. Stir halfway through.
- In a mixing bowl, toss cooked Brussels sprouts with sweet chili sauce and lime juice.
- Serve and enjoy.

Nutritional Value (Amount per Serving):

- Calories 82, Fat 1.6 g, Carbohydrates 16.8 g, Sugar 6 g, Protein 4.1 g, Cholesterol 0 mg

2-Balsamic Brussels Sprouts & Broccoli

Balsamic Brussels Sprouts and Broccoli is a delectable side dish that blends the earthy flavors of Brussels sprouts and broccoli with the sweet and tangy notes of balsamic vinegar.

Preparation Time: 10 minutes

Cooking Time: 10 minutes

Servings: 2

Ingredients:

- 175 g (1 cup) broccoli florets
- 1 tablespoon balsamic vinegar
- 1 tablespoon olive oil
- ¼ teaspoon paprika
- 88 g (1 cup) Brussels sprouts, halved
- Pepper
- Salt

Directions:

- In a bowl, toss broccoli florets, and Brussels sprouts with oil, paprika, vinegar, pepper, and salt.
- Add broccoli and Brussels sprouts into the air fryer basket.
- Cook at 400 F/ 204 C for 8-10 minutes. Stir halfway through.
- Serve and enjoy.

Nutritional Value (Amount per Serving):

- Calories 94, Fat 7.3 g, Carbohydrates 7.1 g, Sugar 1.8 g, Protein 2.8 g, Cholesterol 0 mg

3-Roasted Veggies

Roasted vegetables are a versatile side dish that pairs well with various proteins like chicken, beef, and fish, or can even be enjoyed on their own as a vegetarian option.

Preparation Time: 10 minutes

Cooking Time: 12 minutes

Servings: 4

Ingredients:

- 175 g (1 cup) broccoli florets
- 2 yellow squash, sliced
- 1 red bell pepper, diced
- 1 tablespoon olive oil
- 1/4 onion, sliced
- 1 zucchini, sliced
- 1/2 teaspoon garlic powder
- Pepper
- Salt

Directions:

- In a bowl, toss vegetables with garlic powder, oil, pepper, and salt.
- Add veggie mixture into the air fryer basket.
- Cook at 400 F/ 200 C for 10-12 minutes. Stir halfway through.
- Serve and enjoy.

Nutritional Value (Amount per Serving):

- Calories 76, Fat 3.9 g, Carbohydrates 9.6 g, Sugar 4.8 g, Protein 2.9 g, Cholesterol 0 mg

4-Healthy Balsamic Veggies

Healthy Balsamic Veggies is a nutritious and flavorful side dish that combines a variety of vegetables with the sweet and tangy notes of balsamic vinegar.

Preparation Time: 10 minutes

Cooking Time: 13 minutes

Servings: 4

Ingredients:

- 125 g (8 oz) asparagus, cut woody ends
- 1 yellow squash, sliced
- 170 g (6 oz) cherry tomatoes
- 1/4 cup olive oil
- 125 g (8 oz) mushrooms, halved
- 1 zucchini, sliced
- 1 tablespoon Dijon mustard
- 3 tablespoons soy sauce, low-sodium
- 2 tablespoons coconut sugar
- 1/4 cup balsamic vinegar
- Pepper
- Salt

Directions:

- In a mixing bowl, mix asparagus, mushrooms, tomatoes, zucchini, squash, oil, mustard, soy sauce, coconut sugar, vinegar, pepper, and salt.
- Cover bowl and place in refrigerator for 50 minutes.
- Add veggie mixture into the air fryer basket.
- Cook at 400 F/ 204 C for 13 minutes. Stir halfway through.
- Serve and enjoy.

Nutritional Value (Amount per Serving):

- Calories 186, Fat 13.3 g, Carbohydrates 14.7 g, Sugar 9.5 g, Protein 5.5 g, Cholesterol 0 mg

5-Crispy Eggplant Bites

Crispy Eggplant Bites are a delightful way to enjoy the rich and tender flavor of eggplant with a satisfying crunch.

Preparation Time: 10 minutes

Cooking Time: 15 minutes

Servings: 4

Ingredients:

- 680 g (1 1/2 pounds) eggplant, cut into 1/2-inch chunks
- 1 teaspoon smoked paprika
- 1 teaspoon garlic powder
- 2 tablespoons vegetable broth
- 1/4 teaspoon dried thyme
- 1/2 teaspoon dried oregano
- Pepper
- Salt

Directions:

- In a bowl, toss eggplant with paprika, garlic powder, thyme, oregano, vegetable broth, pepper, and salt.
- Add eggplant pieces into the air fryer basket and cook at 380 F/ 193 C for 15-20 minutes. Stir halfway through.
- Serve and enjoy.

Nutritional Value (Amount per Serving):

- Calories 46, Fat 0.5 g, Carbohydrates 11 g, Sugar 5.4 g, Protein 2.1 g, Cholesterol 0 mg

6-Tasty Cauliflower Florets

Cauliflower Florets is a delicious way to enjoy the nutty and mild flavor of cauliflower with a burst of spices.

Preparation Time: 10 minutes

Cooking Time: 12 minutes

Servings: 4

Ingredients:

- 1 medium cauliflower head, cut into florets
- 1/2 teaspoon turmeric
- 1 teaspoon onion powder
- 2 teaspoons garlic powder
- 1 fresh lime juice
- 2 tablespoons olive oil
- 1 teaspoon chili powder
- 2 teaspoons parsley, chopped
- 1 teaspoon cumin
- Pepper
- Salt

Directions:

- In a bowl, toss cauliflower florets with oil, garlic powder, parsley, chili powder, turmeric, onion powder, cumin, pepper, and salt.
- Add cauliflower florets into the air fryer basket and cook at 400 F/ 204 C for 12 minutes. Stir halfway through.
- Drizzle lime juice over cauliflower florets and serve.

Nutritional Value (Amount per Serving):

- Calories 116, Fat 7.4 g, Carbohydrates 10.9 g, Sugar 4.3 g, Protein 3.4 g, Cholesterol 0 mg

7-Potatoes with Green Beans

Potatoes with green beans are one of the traditional side dishes that is made of a combination of tender, creamy potatoes with crisp, vibrant green beans.

Preparation Time: 10 minutes

Cooking Time: 25 minutes

Servings: 4

Ingredients:

- 453 g (1 pound) potatoes, cut into pieces
- 1 tablespoon olive oil
- ¼ teaspoon onion powder
- ¼ teaspoon paprika
- 1 teaspoon garlic powder
- 226 g (8 oz) green beans, trimmed
- Pepper
- Salt

Directions:

- Preheat the air fryer to 390 F/ 198 C.
- In a bowl, toss green beans, potatoes, oil, paprika, garlic powder, onion powder, pepper, and salt.
- Add green beans and potato mixture into the air fryer basket and cook for 10 minutes.
- Stir well and cook for 10-15 minutes more or until potatoes are tender.
- Serve and enjoy.

Nutritional Value (Amount per Serving):

- Calories 124, Fat 3.7 g, Carbohydrates 22.4 g, Sugar 2.3 g, Protein 3.1 g, Cholesterol 0 mg

8-Roasted Radishes

Roasted radishes are a unique and delicious side dish that transforms peppery and slightly spicy radishes into tender, caramelized bites.

Preparation Time: 10 minutes

Cooking Time: 10 minutes

Servings: 4

Ingredients:

- 453 g (1 pound) radishes, cut into quarters
- 1/2 teaspoon garlic powder
- 2 tablespoons olive oil
- 1/4 teaspoon dried oregano
- 1/2 teaspoon dried parsley
- Pepper
- Salt

Directions:

- In a bowl, toss radishes with garlic powder, oil, dried parsley, oregano, pepper, and salt until well coated.
- Add radishes into the air fryer basket and cook at 350 F/ 176 C for 10 minutes. Stir halfway through.
- Serve and enjoy.

Nutritional Value (Amount per Serving):

- Calories 76, Fat 5.9 g, Carbohydrates 4.2 g, Sugar 2.2 g, Protein 0.9 g, Cholesterol 15 mg

9-Flavorful Green Beans

Flavorful green beans are a nutritious and vibrant side dish that combines the freshness of green beans with delicious flavors.

Preparation Time: 10 minutes

Cooking Time: 20 minutes

Servings: 4

Ingredients:

- 453 g (1 pound) green beans
- 2 tablespoons sesame seeds
- 1 tablespoon coconut sugar
- 1 tablespoon soy sauce, low-sodium
- 1 teaspoon ground ginger
- 1/2 tablespoon honey
- 1 tablespoon sesame oil
- Pepper
- Salt

Directions:

- Add green beans into the air fryer basket and cook at 400 F/ 204 C for 10 minutes.
- In a mixing bowl, add cooked green beans, sesame seeds, coconut sugar, ginger, honey, soy sauce, and oil and toss until well coated.
- Return green beans into the air fryer basket and cook for 10 minutes.
- Serve and enjoy.

Nutritional Value (Amount per Serving):

- Calories 113, Fat 5.8 g, Carbohydrates 14.2 g, Sugar 6 g, Protein 3.2 g, Cholesterol 0 mg

10-Brussels Sprouts & Onion

Brussels sprouts and onions make for a tasty and savory side dish that pairs the earthy flavor of Brussels sprouts with the sweet and caramelized taste of onions.

Preparation Time: 10 minutes

Cooking Time: 10 minutes

Servings: 5

Ingredients:

- 176 g (2 cups) Brussels sprouts, cut in half
- 1 tablespoon balsamic vinegar
- 1 tablespoon olive oil
- ¼ teaspoon garlic powder
- ¼ teaspoon paprika
- 1/2 cup onions, sliced
- Pepper
- Salt

Directions:

- Add Brussels sprouts, onion, garlic powder, paprika, vinegar, oil, pepper, and salt into the bowl and toss well to coat.
- Add Brussels sprouts and onion mixture into the air fryer basket and cook at 350 F/ 176 C for 10 minutes. Stir halfway through.
- Serve and enjoy.

Nutritional Value (Amount per Serving):

- Calories 48, Fat 2.9 g, Carbohydrates 4.3 g, Sugar 1.3 g, Protein 1.3 g, Cholesterol 0 mg

11-Quick Sugar Snap Peas

Quick sugar snap peas are a simple and delicious side dish that showcases the natural sweetness and crisp texture of these delightful vegetables.

Preparation Time: 10 minutes

Cooking Time: 7 minutes

Servings: 4

Ingredients:

- 225 g (8 oz) sugar snap peas, remove end & string
- 2 teaspoons garlic, minced
- 2 tablespoons onion, chopped
- 1 tablespoon olive oil
- 1/2 teaspoon onion powder
- 1/2 tablespoon soy sauce, low-sodium
- Pepper
- Salt

Directions:

- In a mixing bowl, toss sugar snap peas with remaining ingredients until well coated.
- Add sugar snap peas into the air fryer basket.
- Cook at 360 F/ 182 C for 5-7 minutes. Stir halfway through.
- Serve and enjoy.

Nutritional Value (Amount per Serving):

- Calories 52, Fat 3 g, Carbohydrates 5.6 g, Sugar 2.6 g, Protein 1.9 g, Cholesterol 8 mg

12-Greek Vegetables

Greek-style roasted vegetables are a delicious accompaniment to grilled meats, fish, or vegetarian Mediterranean feasts.

Preparation Time: 10 minutes

Cooking Time: 15 minutes

Servings: 6

Ingredients:

- 125 g (1 cup) mushrooms, sliced
- 1 yellow squash, cut into cubes
- 1 zucchini, cut into cubes

- 1/2 onion, diced
- 2 eggplant, cut into cubes
- 2 tablespoons olive oil
- 12 cherry tomatoes
- 2 tablespoons balsamic vinegar
- Pepper
- Salt

Directions:

- Preheat the air fryer to 390 F/ 198 C.
- In a bowl, toss vegetables with oil, vinegar, pepper, and salt.
- Add vegetables into the air fryer basket and cook for 15 minutes. Stir halfway through.
- Serve and enjoy.

Nutritional Value (Amount per Serving):

- Calories 143, Fat 5.6 g, Carbohydrates 22 g, Sugar 12.8 g, Protein 4.9 g, Cholesterol 0 mg

13-Roasted Mushroom Green Beans

Roasted Mushroom Green Beans are a delectable side dish that blends the earthy flavor of mushrooms with the vibrant crunch of green beans.

Preparation Time: 10 minutes

Cooking Time: 20 minutes

Servings: 6

Ingredients:

- 453 g (1 pound) green beans, cut into 2-inch pieces
- 1 small onion, sliced

- 225 g (1/2 pound) mushrooms, sliced
- 2 tablespoons olive oil
- 1 teaspoon Italian seasoning
- Pepper
- Salt

Directions:

- Preheat the air fryer to 375 F/ 190 C.
- In a bowl, toss green beans with the remaining ingredients.
- Add green beans mixture into the air fryer basket and cook for 20 minutes or until cooked. Stir halfway through.
- Serve and enjoy.

Nutritional Value (Amount per Serving):

- Calories 82, Fat 5.1 g, Carbohydrates 7.8 g, Sugar 2.3 g, Protein 2.7 g, Cholesterol 1 mg

14-Tasty Sweet Potato Hash

The Tasty Sweet Potato hash with mushroom is a unique variation of the classic sweet potato hash, incorporating earthy mushrooms for enhanced flavor and depth.

Preparation Time: 10 minutes

Cooking Time: 30 minutes

Servings: 4

Ingredients:

- 4 sweet potatoes, peeled & diced
- 2 tablespoons lime juice
- 1/2 cup bell pepper, chopped
- 1/2 cup onion, chopped
- 1/2 teaspoon dried rosemary
- 1/2 teaspoon dried thyme

- 2 tablespoons olive oil
- 1 cup mushrooms, sliced
- Pepper
- Salt

Directions:

- Preheat the air fryer to 360 F/ 182 C.
- In a mixing bowl, add sweet potatoes, oil, lime juice, rosemary, thyme, bell pepper, onion, mushrooms, pepper, and salt and toss well.
- Add sweet potato mixture into the air fryer basket and cook for 28-30 minutes.
- Serve and enjoy.

Nutritional Value (Amount per Serving):

- Calories 257, Fat 7.5 g, Carbohydrates 45.2 g, Sugar 2.6 g, Protein 3.2 g, Cholesterol 0 mg

15-Simple Okra Fries

These simple okra fries are a healthier alternative to traditional fried okra while still providing a satisfying crunch and a burst of flavor.

Preparation Time: 10 minutes

Cooking Time: 15 minutes

Servings: 4

Ingredients:

- 425 g (15 oz) okra, wash & pat dry
- 1/2 teaspoon garlic powder
- 1 teaspoon chili powder
- 2 tablespoons olive oil
- 1 teaspoon paprika
- Pepper
- Salt

Directions:

- In a bowl, toss the okra with oil, chili powder, paprika, garlic powder, pepper, and salt.
- Add okra into the air fryer basket and cook at 400 F/ 204 C for 15 minutes. Stir halfway through.
- Serve and enjoy.

Nutritional Value (Amount per Serving):

- Calories 103, Fat 7.4 g, Carbohydrates 8.9 g, Sugar 1.8 g, Protein 2.3 g, Cholesterol 0 mg

DESSERT RECIPES

1- Caramelized Cinnamon Bananas

Caramelized cinnamon bananas are a delightful dessert or snack that features ripe bananas cooked in a sweet, caramel-like sauce with a touch of cinnamon.

Preparation Time: 10 minutes

Cooking Time: 8 minutes

Servings: 2

Ingredients:

- 2 ripe bananas, halves
- 1/4 teaspoon cinnamon
- 1 tablespoon butter, melted
- 1/2 teaspoon coconut sugar

Directions:

- Preheat the air fryer to 370 F/ 187 C.
- In a bowl, mix bananas with cinnamon, coconut sugar, and butter.
- Place bananas into the air fryer baking pan.
- Place baking pan into the air fryer basket and cook for 10 minutes. Flip halfway through.
- Serve and enjoy.

Nutritional Value (Amount per Serving):

- Calories 183, Fat 6.2 g, Carbohydrates 31.9 g, Sugar 14.4 g, Protein 1.6 g, Cholesterol 15 mg

2-Healthy Cinnamon Bread

Healthy cinnamon bread is a tasty and nutritious alternative to classic cinnamon bread, often made with ingredients that are lower in sugar, fats, and refined flour.

Preparation Time: 10 minutes

Cooking Time: 30 minutes

Servings: 8

Ingredients:

- 3 eggs
- 1/4 cup cinnamon toast crunch cereal, crushed
- 57 g (1/4 cup) butter, melted
- 1/4 cup Swerve
- 28 g (1/4 cup) coconut flour
- 1 teaspoon cinnamon
- 1 teaspoon vanilla
- 150 g (1 1/4 cups) almond flour

Directions:

- Preheat the air fryer to 350 F/ 176 C.
- In a bowl, whisk butter and sweetener. Add eggs and vanilla and whisk well.
- Add coconut flour, cinnamon, and almond flour and mix well.
- Add crushed cereal and fold well.
- Pour batter into the greased air fryer baking pan.
- Place baking pan into the air fryer basket and cook for 30 minutes.
- Slice and serve.

Nutritional Value (Amount per Serving):

- Calories 126, Fat 10 g, Carbohydrates 4.8 g, Sugar 0.8 g, Protein 3.7 g, Cholesterol 77 mg

3-Peanut Butter Brownies

Peanut Butter Brownies are a delectable dessert that blends the rich, chocolatey goodness of brownies with the creamy, nutty flavor of peanut butter.

Preparation Time: 10 minutes

Cooking Time: 25 minutes

Servings: 16

Ingredients:

- 3 eggs
- 67 g (1/3 cup) unsweetened chocolate chips
- 258 g (1 cup) peanut butter
- 3/4 cup Swerve
- 50 g (1/2 cup) unsweetened cocoa powder
- 100 g (1 cup) almond flour

Directions:

- In a bowl, whisk eggs with peanut butter and sweetener.
- Add almond flour and cocoa powder and mix until well combined.
- Add chocolate chips and fold well.
- Pour batter into the greased air fryer baking pan.
- Place baking pan into the air fryer basket and cook at 300 F/ 148 C for 25 minutes.
- Slice and serve.

Nutritional Value (Amount per Serving):

- Calories 172, Fat 13.8 g, Carbohydrates 8.4 g, Sugar 3.7 g, Protein 7.3 g, Cholesterol 32 mg

4-Banana Chocolate Brownie

Banana chocolate brownies are a delightful fusion of the sweet and moist characteristics of ripe bananas with the rich, chocolaty goodness of brownies.

Preparation Time: 10 minutes

Cooking Time: 8 minutes

Servings: 6

Ingredients:

- 1 banana, mashed
- 1/3 cup chocolate whey protein powder
- 150 g (1 1/2 cups) almond flour
- 1 teaspoon vanilla
- 28 g (1/4 cup) walnuts, chopped
- 50 g (1/4 cup) unsweetened chocolate chips
- 1/2 teaspoon baking soda
- 3 tablespoons butter, melted
- 1/4 teaspoon salt

Directions:

- Add all ingredients except chocolate chips and walnuts into the bowl and mix until well combined.
- Add chocolate chips and walnuts and fold well.
- Pour batter into the greased air fryer baking pan.
- Place the pan into the air fryer basket and cook for 8 minutes.
- Slice and serve.

Nutritional Value (Amount per Serving):

- Calories 184, Fat 14.6 g, Carbohydrates 11 g, Sugar 6.5 g, Protein 4.7 g, Cholesterol 19 mg

5-Tasty Cookie Balls

Tasty cookie balls are a delightful, easy-to-make treat that satisfies your sweet tooth with their delicious bite-sized texture.

Preparation Time: 10 minutes

Cooking Time: 10 minutes

Servings: 10

Ingredients:

- 1 egg
- 1/2 teaspoon cinnamon
- 1 teaspoon vanilla
- 1/4 cup Swerve
- 240 g (1 cup) almond butter
- 50 g (1/4 cup) unsweetened chocolate chips
- 18 g (1/4 cup) shredded coconut, unsweetened
- 25 g (1/4 cup) almond flour

Directions:

- In a bowl, mix the almond butter, egg, almond flour, vanilla, and sweetener until well combined.
- Add shredded coconut, chocolate chips, and cinnamon, and mix well.
- Make small balls from the almond butter mixture and place them into the greased air fryer baking pan.
- Place baking pan into the air fryer basket.
- Cook at 320 F/ 160 C for 10 minutes.
- Serve and enjoy.

Nutritional Value (Amount per Serving):

- Calories 53, Fat 3.6 g, Carbohydrates 3.5 g, Sugar 2.5 g, Protein 1.4 g, Cholesterol 17 mg

6-Chocó Chip Nut Brownies

Chocolate chip nut brownies are a delicious and indulgent dessert that combines the rich, fudgy goodness of brownies with the crunch of chocolate chips and the nuttiness of chopped nuts.

Preparation Time: 10 minutes

Cooking Time: 10 minutes

Servings: 2

Ingredients:

- 1 egg
- 57 g (1/4 cup) butter, melted
- 2 tablespoons cocoa powder
- 1/2 teaspoon baking powder
- 2 tablespoon pecans, chopped
- 2 tablespoons unsweetened chocolate chips
- 1/2 teaspoon vanilla
- 3 tablespoon Swerve
- 32 g (1/3 cup) almond flour

Directions:

- Preheat the air fryer to 350 F/ 176 C.
- In a bowl, mix almond flour, baking powder, sweetener, and cocoa powder.
- Add egg, vanilla, and butter and mix until well combined.
- Add pecans and chocolate chips and fold well.
- Pour batter into the greased air fryer baking pan.
- Place baking pan into the air fryer basket and cook for 10 minutes.
- Slice and serve.

Nutritional Value (Amount per Serving):

- Calories 423, Fat 38 g, Carbohydrates 15.8 g, Sugar 6.4 g, Protein 7.1 g, Cholesterol 145 mg

- Calories 113, Fat 10.2 g, Carbohydrates 4.5 g, Sugar 3 g, Protein 2.6 g, Cholesterol 57 mg

7-Quick Pan Cookie

Quick pan cookies are a delightful dessert to share with friends and family. They are perfect for special occasions, casual get-togethers, or whenever you crave a warm and gooey cookie treat.

Preparation Time: 10 minutes

Cooking Time: 7 minutes

Servings: 4

Ingredients:

- 1 egg
- 1/2 teaspoon baking powder
- 2 tablespoon butter, softened
- 2 tablespoons unsweetened chocolate chips
- 1/2 teaspoon vanilla
- 1/4 cup Swerve
- 50 g (1/2 cup) almond flour

Directions:

- In a bowl, mix almond flour, Swerve, and baking powder.
- Add egg, butter, and vanilla and stir until well combined.
- Add chocolate chips and fold well.
- Pour batter into the greased air fryer baking pan.
- Place baking pan into the air fryer basket and cook at 300 F/ 148 C for 7 minutes.
- Serve and enjoy.

Nutritional Value (Amount per Serving):

8-Moist Pumpkin Cupcakes

Moist pumpkin cupcakes are a delightful seasonal treat that captures the warm and comforting flavors of pumpkin and spices.

Preparation Time: 10 minutes

Cooking Time: 30 minutes

Servings: 10

Ingredients:

- 1 egg
- 300 g (3 cups) almond flour
- 82 g (1/3 cup) unsweetened almond milk
- 76 g (1/3 cup) butter, melted
- 1/2 cup Erythritol
- 1 teaspoon baking soda
- 1 teaspoon vanilla
- 1/8 teaspoon ground cloves
- 60 g (1/4 cup) pumpkin puree
- 1/4 teaspoon ground nutmeg
- 2 teaspoons lemon juice
- 2 teaspoons ground ginger
- 2 teaspoons ground cinnamon
- 1/4 teaspoon salt

Directions:

- In a bowl, mix almond flour, baking soda, cinnamon, ginger, Erythritol, nutmeg, cloves, and salt.
- In a separate bowl, whisk eggs with lemon juice, milk, butter, and pumpkin puree.
- Add egg mixture into the almond flour mixture and mix until well combined.

- Spoon batter into the silicone muffin molds.
- Place muffin molds into the air fryer basket.
- Cook at 300 F/ 148 C for 15 minutes.
- Serve and enjoy.

Nutritional Value (Amount per Serving):

- Calories 118, Fat 11 g, Carbohydrates 15.1 g, Sugar 12.6 g, Protein 2.6 g, Cholesterol 33 mg

9-Easy Pound Cake

Easy pound cake is a satisfying low-carb treat, with the option to experiment with different sweeteners for a different taste.

Preparation Time: 10 minutes

Cooking Time: 25 minutes

Servings: 6

Ingredients:

- 2 eggs
- 1 teaspoon baking powder
- 1 teaspoon vanilla
- 1/2 cup Swerve
- 1 oz cream cheese, softened
- 1/2 cup sour cream
- 57 g (1/4 cup) butter, melted
- 100 g (1 cup) almond flour

Directions:

- In a bowl, mix almond flour, sweetener, and butter.
- Add cream cheese, baking powder, sour cream, egg, and vanilla, and mix until well combined.

- Pour batter into the greased air fryer baking pan.
- Place baking pan into the air fryer basket and cook at 300 F/ 148 C for 25 minutes.
- Slice and serve.

Nutritional Value (Amount per Serving):

- Calories 176, Fat 17.1 g, Carbohydrates 2.7 g, Sugar 0.4 g, Protein 3.9 g, Cholesterol 89 mg

10-Cinnamon Pear Slices

Cinnamon pear slices are a delightful and healthy snack or dessert that combines the natural sweetness of pears with the warmth and aroma of ground cinnamon.

Preparation Time: 10 minutes

Cooking Time: 15 minutes

Servings: 2

Ingredients:

- 1 medium pear, peel, core, and cut into 1/4-inch slices
- 1 tablespoon coconut sugar
- 1/2 teaspoon cinnamon
- 2 tablespoon butter, melted

Directions:

- In a bowl, toss pear slices with coconut sugar, cinnamon, and butter until well coated.
- Add pear slices into the greased air fryer baking pan.
- Place baking pan into the air fryer basket and cook at 340 F/ 171 C for 15 minutes.
- Serve and enjoy.

Nutritional Value (Amount per Serving):

- Calories 163, Fat 11.6 g, Carbohydrates 15.5 g, Sugar 11.2 g, Protein 0.4 g, Cholesterol 31 mg

30-Day Meal Plan

Day 1

- ➢ Breakfast-Healthy Vegetable Frittata
- ➢ Lunch-Tasty Cauliflower Florets
- ➢ Snack- Crunchy Chickpeas
- ➢ Dinner-Dijon Chicken Breasts

Day 2

- ➢ Breakfast-Crustless Quiche
- ➢ Lunch-Spicy Prawns
- ➢ Snack- Roasted Cashews
- ➢ Dinner-Easy Balsamic Lamb Chops

Day 3

- ➢ Breakfast-Veggie Egg Cups
- ➢ Lunch-Roasted Mushroom Green Beans
- ➢ Snack- Crispy Potato Bites
- ➢ Dinner-Herb Lemon Lamb Chops

Day 4

- ➢ Breakfast-Baked Banana Oatmeal
- ➢ Lunch-Shrimp & Veggies
- ➢ Snack- Delicious Broccoli Tots
- ➢ Dinner-Garlic Mint Lamb Chops

Day 5

- ➢ Breakfast-Sweet Potato Hash
- ➢ Lunch-Roasted Veggies
- ➢ Snack- Perfect Carrot Fries
- ➢ Dinner-Dijon Pork Chops & Brussels Sprouts

Day 6

- ➢ Breakfast-Spinach Egg Bites
- ➢ Lunch-Balsamic Brussels Sprouts & Broccoli
- ➢ Snack- Spicy Sweet Potato Wedges
- ➢ Dinner-Crispy Parmesan Pork Chops

Day 7

- ➢ Breakfast-Perfect Oatmeal Bites
- ➢ Lunch-Tasty Sweet Potato Hash
- ➢ Snack- Crispy Zucchini Fritters
- ➢ Dinner-Flavorful Pesto Chicken Breasts

Day 8

- ➢ Breakfast-Quick & Easy Granola
- ➢ Lunch-Brussels Sprouts & Onion
- ➢ Snack- Easy Hasselback Potatoes
- ➢ Dinner-Marinated Chicken

Day 9

- ➢ Breakfast-Blueberry Muffins
- ➢ Lunch-Healthy Balsamic Veggies
- ➢ Snack- Healthy Veggie Skewers
- ➢ Dinner-Juicy Turkey Breast

Day 10

- ➢ Breakfast-Tasty Greek Omelet
- ➢ Lunch-Potatoes with Green Beans

- ➢ Snack- Crispy Cabbage Patties
- ➢ Dinner-Marinated Sirloin Steak

Day 11

- ➢ Breakfast-Healthy Vegetable Frittata
- ➢ Lunch-Chili Lime Brussels sprouts

- ➢ Snack- Crunchy Chickpeas
- ➢ Dinner-Curried Fish Fillets

Day 12

- ➢ Breakfast-Crustless Quiche
- ➢ Lunch-Tasty Sweet Potato Hash

- ➢ Snack- Roasted Cashews
- ➢ Dinner-Dijon Chicken Breasts

Day 13

- ➢ Breakfast-Veggie Egg Cups
- ➢ Lunch- Brussels Sprouts & Onion

- ➢ Snack- Crispy Potato Bites
- ➢ Dinner-Salmon with Veggies

Day 14

- ➢ Breakfast-Baked Banana Oatmeal
- ➢ Lunch-Pesto Scallops
- ➢ Snack- Delicious Broccoli Tots
- ➢ Dinner-Balsamic Dijon Pork Chops

Day 15

- ➢ Breakfast-Sweet Potato Hash
- ➢ Lunch-Greek Vegetables
- ➢ Snack- Perfect Carrot Fries
- ➢ Dinner-Greek Salmon Fillets

Day 16

- ➢ Breakfast-Spinach Egg Bites
- ➢ Lunch- Brussels Sprouts & Onion

- ➢ Snack- Spicy Sweet Potato Wedges
- ➢ Dinner-Tasty Tuna Steaks

Day 17

- ➢ Breakfast-Perfect Oatmeal Bites
- ➢ Lunch- Potatoes with Green Beans

- ➢ Snack- Crispy Zucchini Fritters
- ➢ Dinner-Crispy Crusted Pork Chops

Day 18

- ➢ Breakfast-Quick & Easy Granola
- ➢ Lunch- Chili Lime Brussels sprouts

- ➢ Snack- Easy Hasselback Potatoes
- ➢ Dinner-Asian Salmon

Day 19

- ➢ Breakfast-Blueberry Muffins
- ➢ Lunch- Greek Vegetables
- ➢ Snack- Healthy Veggie Skewers
- ➢ Dinner- Dijon Chicken Breasts

Day 20

- ➢ Breakfast-Tasty Greek Omelet
- ➢ Lunch- Healthy Balsamic Veggies

- ➢ Snack- Crispy Cabbage Patties
- ➢ Dinner-Juicy Flank Steak

Day 21

- ➢ Breakfast-Healthy Vegetable Frittata
- ➢ Lunch-Tasty Sweet Potato Hash

- ➢ Snack- Crunchy Chickpeas

➢ Dinner- Curried Fish Fillets

Day 22

➢ Breakfast-Crustless Quiche
➢ Lunch- Cheese Herb Shrimp
➢ Snack- Roasted Cashews
➢ Dinner-Quick Lamb Chops

Day 23

➢ Breakfast-Veggie Egg Cups
➢ Lunch- Healthy Balsamic Veggies

➢ Snack- Crispy Potato Bites
➢ Dinner-Juicy Lamb Chops

Day 24

➢ Breakfast-Baked Banana Oatmeal
➢ Lunch- Pesto Scallops
➢ Snack- Delicious Broccoli Tots
➢ Dinner-Garlic Herb Pork Chops

Day 25

➢ Breakfast-Sweet Potato Hash
➢ Lunch- Greek Vegetables
➢ Snack- Perfect Carrot Fries
➢ Dinner- Dijon Chicken Breasts

Day 26

➢ Breakfast-Spinach Egg Bites
➢ Lunch- Brussels Sprouts & Onion

➢ Snack- Spicy Sweet Potato Wedges
➢ Dinner-Flavors Pork Tenderloin

Day 27

➢ Breakfast-Perfect Oatmeal Bites
➢ Lunch-Cheese Herb Shrimp
➢ Snack- Crispy Zucchini Fritters

➢ Dinner- Salmon with Veggies

Day 28

➢ Breakfast-Quick & Easy Granola
➢ Lunch- Potatoes with Green Beans

➢ Snack- Easy Hasselback Potatoes
➢ Dinner-Lemon Pepper Fish Fillets

Day 29

➢ Breakfast-Blueberry Muffins
➢
➢ Lunch- Chili Lime Brussels sprouts

➢ Snack- Healthy Veggie Skewers
➢ Dinner-Juicy Lamb Chops

Day 30

➢ Breakfast-Tasty Greek Omelet
➢ Lunch- Greek Vegetables
➢ Snack- Crispy Cabbage Patties
➢ Dinner-Marinated Salmon with Veggies

Conclusion

Thank you for joining us on the journey towards healthier and more flavorful eating through the "Diabetic Air Fryer Cookbook for Beginners." Managing diabetes can be a challenge; however, your determination, creativity, and commitment to your well-being have made it easier. In this cookbook, we have explored the magic of the air fryer, transforming ordinary ingredients into extraordinary meals that not only satisfy your taste buds but also support your blood sugar control. We have shown that diabetes-friendly cooking doesn't mean sacrificing flavor; it means discovering new ways to enhance it.

This cookbook has become a trusted companion in your kitchen, inspiring you to try new recipes, experiment with ingredients, and find joy in the art of cooking. Remember that managing diabetes is not a one-size-fits-all journey. Your unique tastes and preferences should always be celebrated as part of your diabetes management plan.

As you continue to explore the world of diabetes-friendly cuisine, may you find confidence and empowerment in your culinary skills. Let the recipes within these pages serve as a foundation for your own culinary adventures, and may your meals always be a source of nourishment, delight, and good health.

Thank you for prioritizing your well-being and allowing this cookbook to be a part of your journey. Whether you're cooking for yourself or sharing meals with loved ones, may every dish be a celebration of good food, good health, and the joy of living life to the fullest.

Wishing you an abundance of delicious moments and continued success in managing your diabetes. Bon appétit and be well.

Regards,

Isabella Reynold

References

Algoblan, A. S., Al-Alfi, M. A., & Khan, M. Z. (2014). Mechanism linking diabetes mellitus and obesity. Diabetes, Metabolic Syndrome and Obesity: Targets and Therapy, 587. https://doi.org/10.2147/dmso.s67400

Causes and risk factors | NHLBI, NIH. (2022, March 24). NHLBI, NIH. https://www.nhlbi.nih.gov/health/overweight-and-obesity/causes

Diabetes diet: Create your healthy-eating plan. (2023, April 13). Mayo Clinic. https://www.mayoclinic.org/diseases-conditions/diabetes/in-depth/diabetes-diet/art-20044295

Food and diet. (2016, April 8). Obesity Prevention Source. https://www.hsph.harvard.edu/obesity-prevention-source/obesity-causes/diet-and-weight/

Meal planning for Managing your diabetes - Health Encyclopedia - University of Rochester Medical Center. (n.d.). https://www.urmc.rochester.edu/encyclopedia/content.aspx?contenttypeid=85&contentid=P00346

National Library of Medicine. (n.d.). Diabetic diet. MedlinePlus. https://medlineplus.gov/diabeticdiet.html

News-Medical.net. (2023, January 23). Obesity and diabetes. https://www.news-medical.net/health/Obesity-and-Diabetes.aspx

Professional, C. C. M. (n.d.). Diabetes. Cleveland Clinic. https://my.clevelandclinic.org/health/diseases/7104-diabetes

Ryan, A. (2023a, April 12). Are air fryers healthy? https://www.medicalnewstoday.com/articles/324849

Uk, D. (n.d.). 10 tips for healthy eating with diabetes. Diabetes UK. https://www.diabetes.org.uk/guide-to-diabetes/enjoy-food/eating-with-diabetes/10-ways-to-eat-well-with-diabetes

Printed in Great Britain
by Amazon